YOUNG
BUT NOT THAT
YOUNG

Lessons from Paul for
Timothy, Titus, and Today's Twenties

by Hal Hammons

ONESTONE
BIBLICAL RESOURCES

Published by:
One Stone Press
979 Lovers Lane
Bowling Green, KY 42103

Printed in the United States of America

ISBN 13: 978-1-941422-44-1

Supplemental Materials Available:

~ Answer Key

~ Downloadable PDF

www.onestone.com

1.800.428.0121

www.onestone.com

CONTENTS

Dedication

To Taylor and Kylie Hammons,
My best students, and my greatest achievement.

Foreword

I grew up in Austin, Texas, many years ago. My father, a native of the Hill Country, would take the family out to his hometown of Spicewood, in Burnet County, most Saturdays so we could spend time with my grandparents. We helped in their garden, did chores, that sort of thing. I didn't especially enjoy it. I liked driving the tractor, and I didn't mind feeding the cattle too much. But I fancied myself a city boy. Burnet County was a bit too lowbrow.

So when I saw the plain white leaflet on my parents' coffee table every month entitled "PLAIN TALK," I just associated it with that funny little preacher in Burnet County, just down the road from Mimmee and Pawpaw. Another old guy. A country bumpkin. His paper was two legal-sized pages folded in half. No graphics. No color. No staple. Not worth my time. Not when there's a new issue of The Flash calling me.

Today as I type I am staring across my office at my bound volumes of "PLAIN TALK," comprising two decades' worth of some of the best writing on Bible topics I have ever read. If my office were on fire and I could save only one armful of books, "PLAIN TALK" would be at the top of the stack.

Several years ago I took my family back to Burnet County to visit my parents, who had retired there. At worship services Sunday morning, I made a point of taking my daughters, then both pre-teens, up to the second pew on the right side to meet the funny little man. I knew he wouldn't be with us much longer, and I knew the day would come when Taylor and Kylie would ask me if they ever met him. I wanted to be able to tell them they had, and that I wished they could have known him better.

I miss Robert Turner very, very much. In retrospect, I wish I had spent every weekend in Burnet County, sitting at his feet. I certainly wish I had read "PLAIN TALK" more diligently in my formative years. But I didn't.

It bothers me when I see the same disregard for elders in today's youth that I remember from my youth. But I do not fear. I know the lessons are sinking in, no matter how much they want to pretend they are not. They are growing more than I realize, more than they realize. And if they manage to survive adolescence with their faith intact, with a general appreciation for Biblical authority and humility before God, they will likely do as I did — catch up as quickly as they can, find respect for the previous generation a bit later than should have been the case, and then go on to become frustrated at the stubborn, headstrong nature of their own children. God willing, we will continue the aggravation for many years to come.

I am no Robert Turner. But I want to play my Timothy to his Paul. As the apostle wrote in 2 Timothy 2:2, one generation teaches the next generation to teach the generation after that. This book is intended to keep the train of teachers and students going a little while longer. My prayer is that it will find its way into the hands of young men and women who have the desire to serve in the Lord's church but are struggling a bit to find their place. My prayer also is that they will find that place and embrace it with a bit less resistance than I put up when I was in their place so many years ago.

As Paul said long ago, "Be imitators of me, just as I also am of Christ" (1 Corinthians 11:1).

A special thanks goes out to the Cedar Park church of Christ in Cedar Park, Texas, for making "PLAIN TALK" available at no cost to anyone who likes a good story and a great tutorial in the faith. If you like what you read of Brother Turner's work here, visit http://www.wordsfitlyspoken.org/plain_talk/ for more, as well as outstanding contributions from Dan Shipley, Jim Everett, and Joe Fitch.

Brotherly, and fatherly,

Hal Hammons
Pace, Florida
July 2016

SOUND DOCTRINE

"In pointing out these things to the brethren, you will be a good servant of Christ Jesus, constantly nourished on the words of the faith and of the sound doctrine which you have been following."

— 1 Timothy 4:6

Paul mentions "strange doctrines" (1 Timothy 1:3) before "sound teaching" (1 Timothy 1:10) or "sound doctrine (1 Timothy 4:6) in his first letter to his friend and apprentice. But if we are to understand "strange doctrine" properly, we must first understand "sound doctrine."

"Sound" means healthy, solid, reliable. A sound piece of wood has no defects or internal rot; it will make for a good piece of furniture, support beam or baseball bat. "Sound" doctrine works the same way. It is tested. It is consistent. It can be counted on to accomplish the task for which it is intended.

That task, of course, is the construction of a Christian. If we are to be made over into the image of Christ (Romans 8:29, Galatians 2:20), we must follow the instructions. The most important part of the instructions is a picture of the completed project, which we have in the life of Jesus Himself (1 Peter 2:21). If we follow the words He gave to His apostles and other inspired writers, constantly looking to His life to see if we are drifting, we can have confidence that God's will can and shall be accomplished in our lives.

No part of His doctrine is false. No part of His doctrine is superfluous. Walking by faith means accepting that God's plan for our lives is completely and understandably laid out for us in the Bible. Reading the Bible is how we "ask of God ... in faith, nothing doubting" regarding the wisdom we need every day (James 1:5-6). If we trust in Him, we will trust in His word. If we trust in His word, we will abide in His teaching revealed in it.

Further Reading

Galatians 1:6-10

Ephesians 4:5

2 Thessalonians 2:13-15

Jude 3

Is there a difference between "the faith" and "the sound doctrine?"

_____

_____

_____

Doug says ...

I get it already. Establish Bible authority for all we do. Learn the lessons of the past. The truth, the whole truth, and nothing but the truth. The fact of the matter is, all I see is Christians of different doctrinal stripes who can't get along. I can't help thinking a little more talk about brotherly love and a little less about "soundness" would go a long way toward mending the fences that have separated us all this time.

What would you say to Doug?

_____

_____

_____

A Lesson from your Bible — Acts 19:1-7

Paul happened upon some disciples when he went back to Ephesus on his third preaching trip. Having preached there only briefly, and that about a year previously, he surely was curious to find what sort of disciples they would be. But these had been baptized through the authority of John the Baptist, not Jesus Himself. John's baptism, though effective in its time and for its purposes (Luke 3:1-6), was not "the power of God for salvation to everyone who believes" (Romans 1:16) that Paul had been preaching. Yes, they were motivated. Yes, they were somewhat informed. Yes, they seemed on the surface to have done what Jesus had required. But they were not there yet.

If baptism is the act through which we are introduced into a relationship with Jesus (Galatians 3:27), then we certainly want to make sure we are baptized correctly. If baptism in the wrong name is a failure to submit to the call of the gospel as described in Acts 2:38, then we should have no confidence in "baptism" that is performed in the wrong way (i.e., by sprinkling or pouring instead of immersion). Nor should we trust in an act called "baptism" that was for some purpose other than God's purpose—the removal of sins

(1 Peter 3:21, Acts 22:16, etc.). We may say such actions are "a different kind of baptism" and put a check in the Mark 16:16 box. But for the purposes of sound doctrine, true discipleship, and pursuing the will of God, is there really "a different kind of baptism" in God's eyes? And if not, should there be one in ours?

It's not a matter of whether God is capable of saving us any other way. It is a matter of whether we want to submit to His will. Is it the attitude of a true disciple to do things his way, being assured in his mind that He will let us get away with it? Or is that the attitude of a rebellious and ungrateful child?

At what point does a person become "a Christian"? What is his state prior to that event? _____

_____

_____

A Lesson from your Elder

I'm sure you're tired of the rest of the old folks and me rehashing basic Bible principles. You think you have these down pat, that you don't need to review them. But you're wrong.

People don't fall from the faith because of fast-talking false teachers; they fall because they are not rooted in the truth. So "Buy the truth, and do not sell it" (Proverbs 23:23).

I love you, and I'm praying for you.

> *O God and Father above,*
> *Help these young Christians learn to truly*
> *revere Your word. Help them to give it a*
> *permanent place in their hearts, and help it*
> *to grow and flourish there.*
> *In Jesus' name,*
> *Amen.*

From PLAIN TALK

They were cushioned in tissue and carefully preserved in a beautiful gilded box. Three tightly rolled balls of—"grey hair?—no, on closer inspection I saw they were spirals of feathers. The largest was about two inches in diameter, and the others were little more than an inch across.

I wanted you to see my brother's crowns," the little lady said; and she handled the box with obvious concern—almost reverence. "They were found in his pillow after he died."

She must have noticed the puzzled look which crossed my face, for she continued, "You know, most men never make a 'profession' but, well—his wife waited for some time before she would open his pillow. Then, when she did, this is what she found!" The drawn, questioning look, was now replaced with a look of confidence.

The implication was obvious. Although her deceased brother had never "professed" Christ, she based her hopes for his eternal well-being on the fact that these balls of feathers—likely from the washing of the pillows, or drawn into place by the curve and weight distribution common to each feather—had been found in the pillow on which he had slept.

I suppose I was speechless at the absurdity of the whole matter, and I did not wish to hurt the dear little woman's feelings; but when her husband said, somewhat apologetically that he had his doubts about such a thing, I hastened to "back him up."

The lady fingered the feathers lightly, smoothing them into place and slowly closed the lid over them. I could not help but feel a deep compassion for her as she put them away. Grasping at straws—or feathers!! It is so common and so hopeless...

It made me sad—it made me angry! Looking back on the whole affair, I realize that a catalogue of mixed emotions raced through my system, and I can't help but wonder if the desire to teach people the way of life in Christ—one of those feelings most certainly present—will be a strong and enduring one, and push me on to DO something about such superstition.

That woman believes, or thinks she believes, that the Bible is the Word of God. What a commentary on the effect of emotional, social religion, that rejects plain objective teaching.

From PLAIN TALK, August 1969, pg. 8

STRANGE DOCTRINE

"As I urged you upon my departure for Macedonia, remain on at Ephesus so that you may instruct certain men not to teach strange doctrines."

— 1 Timothy 1:3

Paul knew the church at Ephesus well. He was the first to preach the gospel there, although he did not remain to establish a church (Acts 18:19-21). He preached there for more than two years (Acts 19:8-10). He wrote an epistle to them that was preserved for us today. And he made a point of exhorting the elders there to maintain the faith when he passed through the area on his way to Jerusalem and prison (Acts 20:17-38). In fact, he told them, "Be on guard for yourselves," and that "savage wolves" would afflict the flock while under their oversight (Acts 20:28-30). It seems that Paul was entrusting Timothy to continue the work Paul had begun and been forced to abandon.

Might Phygelus and Hermogenes (2 Timothy 1:5) be among those "certain men" who were present in Ephesus and holding false doctrines? Were perhaps Hymenaeus and Alexander (1 Timothy 1:20) others with whom Paul had already dealt? And if so, why did he bring one task to completion and not the other?

Notice, though, that Paul warns of those who might teach false doctrine, not just those who hold them. It is worth the attention of the elders if a member holds a position contrary to the truth of the gospel. If it is determined that he misunderstood the gospel from the beginning, his conversion experience (and consequently, his standing with the church) might be called into question. Elders will use their judgment as to how to deal with a brother or sister in Christ who is mistaken on a doctrinal point that is not a bone of contention with the body.

One who teaches a false doctrine is to be handled much differently. Paul repeatedly in these letters emphasizes the need for elders to "refute those who contradict" (Titus 1:9) and even to eventually "Reject a factious man" (Titus 3:10).

Further Reading

Acts 17:11

1 John 4:1

Galatians 2:11-14

Do "strange doctrines" come in degrees of severity? Explain.

_____

_____

_____

Erica says...

A friend of mine gave me a book for my birthday. It is a fictionalized account of the story of Ruth. It helped me put myself in Ruth's position, feeling what she must have felt during a trying part of her life. I know reading about Ruth like that is not the same as studying the Bible. But one of my Christian friends said she thinks it can do more harm than good. Is that true?

What would you say to Erica?

_____

_____

_____

A Lesson from Your Bible—Jeremiah 28

Jeremiah had enough troubles just preaching an unpopular message to an unreceptive nation. He knew, because God had told him, the people would not respond well when he told them God's plan for dealing with the Babylonian threat — surrender immediately, go quietly, and trust in the mercy of the most ruthless dictator in the world.

Making it worse, however, were "prophets" who spoke in the name of God just as Jeremiah did — only they did not bring the same message as Jeremiah. One such man was Hananiah. He specifically refuted Jeremiah's prophecy that the people would remain in captivity for 70 years (Jeremiah 25:11), saying instead that everything Nebuchadnezzar had taken away, goods and people alike, would return within two years.

Jeremiah, no doubt in a mocking tone, approved of the good news Hananiah gave. But he reminded Hananiah and the people that the prophet truly sent by God was the one whose prophecies came to fulfillment (Deuteronomy 18:22). Undeterred, Hananiah took the yoke Jeremiah had been wearing to symbolize Babylonian oppression and broke it before all, saying in the name of God that the yoke of Nebuchadnezzar would be broken.

The difference between the two, of course, was that God was speaking through Jeremiah. And He told him Hananiah would die within the year for having "counseled rebellion against the LORD." Jeremiah's prophecy came true, which should have put the fear of God, literally, into the hearts of his listeners. Unfortunately, they continued to rebel as Hananiah had, and eventually, they were destroyed as he was.

Why do people prefer man's lies to God's truth? How can we help them see the light if they are determined to remain in darkness?

_____

_____

_____

A Lesson from Your Elder

There is not a bogeyman in every closet, and not every church has a false teacher that needs to be ferreted out. But false doctrine is not hypothetical. It is as old as the truth. And it's not enough to get ready for it once it appears. You need to be ready ahead of time. It's not enough to love the truth. You must "hate every false way" (Psalm 119:104)

War stories of the church in previous generations can be boring, granted. But forewarned is forearmed. So I'm fore-warning you. Get ready. It's coming.

I love you, and I'm praying for you.

> *O God and Father above,*
> *Use your word to give these young Chris-*
> *tians the wisdom they will need in coming*
> *years to guide themselves, their families, and*
> *the church through hard times.*
> *In Jesus' name,*
> *Amen.*

From PLAIN TALK

Give Me That Old Time Religion

"Therefore if thou bring thy gift to the altar, and there rememberest that thy brother hath aught against thee; leave there thy gift before the altar, and go thy way; first be reconciled to thy brother, and then come and offer thy gift." Matt. 5:23-f

You may have observed this is no longer "old-time" -- it is positively antique. How long has it been since you have seen this kind of respect for God, and the honest forth-rightness this practice demands?

Jesus was teaching that we must have clean heart and hands to properly approach the throne of God. You are obligated to go to the brother who feels you have wronged him and make an honest attempt to rectify matters. You must correct your error in order to worship God acceptably.

"But my brother is in error," you say. "I must have no company with him." What self-righteousness, this is.

Did you make an effort to redeem your brother? (Matt. 18:15-17) When you severed relationship with him, was it in a sincere effort to teach him truth? (1 Cor.5:5 2 Cor. 2:6-11) Or, (be honest with yourself) did you accept some third party's appraisal of the matter, get in a "huff", and decide to "stamp out the opposition"?

Are you proud of yourself for your prejudicial stubbornness? For shame! Paul wrote, "If any man obey not our word by this epistle, note that man, and have no company with him, that he may be ashamed. Yet count him not as an enemy, but admonish him as a brother." (2 Thes. 3:14-15)

We are not to "company" with evil, i.e., to condone, or be a partaker in error; but any honest man can see the vast difference in this and a "nose-in-the-air" attitude so often confused with Christian discipline.

Old Time Religion, indeed! When did Jesus; the Apostles, or any other approved Christian of the N.T. ever refuse to answer honest questions or engage in careful study of divine matters? They would have us do unto others as we would be done by.

Think this over before you next worship God. Must we wait to meet our brother before Christ, the Judge?

From PLAIN TALK, March 1964, pg. 1

HUMILITY

"It is a trustworthy statement, deserving full acceptance, that Christ Jesus came into the world to save sinners, among whom I am foremost of all."

— 1 Timothy 2:15

Occasionally Paul gets dragged, kicking and screaming, into flashing his resume. In 2 Corinthians 11:21-29, he is compelled to provide a quick synopsis of all the sufferings he had endured for the cause of Christ. In Philippians 3:2-6, he describes his upbringing in Judaism by way of proving that his credibility on the subject of the Law of Moses and the hope of Abraham were unmatched by any of his critics. Generally, though, he minimizes such things. In fact, he goes on to say in Philippians 3 that he was glad to be rid of the reputation of which he was once so proud. He wanted to "be found in Him, not having a righteousness of my own derived from the Law but that which is through faith in Christ, the righteousness which comes from God on the basis of faith" (Philippians 3:9).

For Paul, the most important factor was always what God had done for him through Jesus, not what he had done for God through Jesus. Since neither His blessings nor our shortcomings can be counted, we are always inclined to give glory to God instead of craving or courting it for ourselves. In fact, the gospel message seems to have been specifically designed to keep us from bragging too much about our part in it.

As a result, we should exercise a great deal of caution when we begin measuring ourselves favorably against our brethren or our neighbors. In the end, Jesus is the only great One in this story. Whatever success we may be able to find in His service is only a testimony to the power and patience of our Savior; only He could use instruments as poor as this to accomplish anything worthwhile at all.

How do we make sure our light shines for the world to see while still maintaining an attitude of humility?

_____

_____

_____

Further Reading

Philippians 3:7-14

Luke 18:9-14

1 Corinthians 1:26-31

Doug says ...

I recently spent a week at a "singing school." A big part of it was song leader training. I feel like I learned a lot, and I know I am going to be more effective in my leadership. But most of our men, frankly, have no idea what they are doing. They can't pitch properly, direct properly, or even choose appropriate songs. I would like to help, but I doubt they'd want to learn—even if they were to take me seriously, which they probably won't.

What would you say to Doug?

_____

_____

_____

A Lesson from Your Bible—Daniel 4

Nebuchadnezzar had everything. He reigned over the greatest city in the world — a city at the core of an empire that was in the process of conquering most of the known world. He is said to have presided over the construction of the fabled Hanging Gardens, one of the so-called "Seven Wonders of the Ancient World." And he did not hesitate to give credit where he thought it due: "Is this not Babylon the great, which I myself have built as a royal residence by the might of my power and for the glory of my majesty?" (Daniel 4:30).

This boasting was despite the warning given to him by his trusted adviser, the prophet Daniel. After hearing of the king's strange dream of a great tree in the forest, Daniel foretold that Nebuchadnezzar, like the tree, would be brought down. He would be made to live as an animal, Daniel said, "until you recognize that the Most High is ruler over the realm of mankind and bestows it on whomever He wishes" (Daniel 2:25). Whatever accomplishments Nebuchadnezzar had made or would make in the future was a gift from God. He, as Nebuchadnezzar finally came to confess, is the One of whom it can be said, "For His dominion is an everlasting dominion, and His kingdom endures from generation to generation" (Daniel 4:34).

God could have used anyone to elevate Babylon. The proof was provided when Nebuchadnezzar was rendered completely incompetent, only to return to his senses and find his kingdom just as it was. We may be great in our assessment of circumstances. But in truth, many factors over which we had little or no control contributed — to say nothing of the generosity of God Himself. To brag is to take all the glory for ourselves, which is a "bragging right" to which we are not entitled.

Whether Nebuchadnezzar ever came to true faith in the God of heaven, or whether his pride allowed him to retain it, is not stated in the text. But for a moment at least, he was moved to "exalt and honor the King of heaven, for all His works are true and His ways just, and He is able to humble those who walk in pride" (Daniel 4:37). May we learn our lesson easier and more painlessly than he did — and then retain it for life.

In what circumstances are we likely to allow our pride to get the better of us?

_____

_____

_____

A Lesson from Your Elder

I once was young and arrogant, too. Thankfully, I survived. In retrospect, I have to wonder how (by the grace of God and my patient brethren, I can only assume). I thought I had all the answers; now, having far more wisdom and knowledge than I did then, I realize I am only barely beginning to appreciate the questions.

Talk less. Listen more. You may learn that what you were so desperate to say was in fact not worth saying at all.

I love you, and I'm praying for you.

> *O God and Father above,*
> *Give these young Christians time*
> *and opportunity to grow in knowledge*
> *and wisdom. Give them the honesty to*
> *recognize their flaws, and the courage*
> *to address them.*
> *In Jesus' name,*
> *Amen.*

From PLAIN TALK

This touching letter is one of the true rewards we receive for writing PLAIN TALK. It covers bitterness (see editorial page) with a gentle cloak.

_____

"I surely did enjoy reading "To See Ourselves" in your May publication of PLAIN TALK. It has helped me to see that I'm not as I should be: first, as a Christian, and secondly, as a preacher's wife. I found myself griping about where we live and not having the right attitude at all. Trivial matters upset me, and though I was aware my attitude was not Christian, I would slip back into my old rut.

"This article has made me sit up and take notice of myself inside and out, and I know I can't act like a Christian on the outside and feel resentful inside. _____ has been very wonderful and patient with me. I'd have thrown me right out the door for acting so childish.

"How can I, being evil, speak good things." That does answer itself doesn't it? And you know, the thought never entered my mind to put "I" in the place of "ye." Isn't it strange how we always think He is talking to others than ourselves?

"I will read this article again and again. Thank you for writing it."

_____

To Which We Replied:
Bro. Jones, Stetson, size 7 1-2; Walked the streets of Podunk, shook hands with the Mayor, had coffee with the Chief of Police.

Sist. Jones, sun-bonnet, small; Washed the clothes, changed the baby, visited the neighbor.

Bro. Jones, 42 long, Hart-Schaffner and Marx; Mounted the rostrum, roared like a lion, acknowledged the applause.

Sist. Jones, gingham, size 12; Sat with the neighbor, introduced her to the Lord, prayed and sang.

Bro. Jones, striding in front, approached the gate. "My wife will be here presently," he said. "Meantime, I'll be fitted with my robe and crown."

But the attendant replied, "Sorry Sir! There is but one outfit prepared: A small crown, and one white robe, size 12."

From PLAIN TALK, June 1966, pg. 8

TRANQUILITY

"First of all then, I urge that entreaties and prayers, petitions and thanksgivings, be made on behalf of all men, for kings and all who are in authority, so that we may lead a tranquil and quiet life in all godliness and dignity."

— 1 Timothy 2:1-2

Young people hate boredom. They want things to happen. Excitement, good. Ordinary, bad. Shake things up. Always shake things up. It's the natural course of progression for people who haven't figured out yet who they are. It is assumed that, at some point in the (distant) future, things will normalize. But until then, it's one big roller coaster ride — and the wilder and crazier, the better.

This creates a bit of a problem for young Christians, who (in theory, at least) have already decided who they are. They are children of the King, disciples of the Master. Their life is an unceasing pursuit of the goal — and the prize that awaits such ones in the end (Philippians 3:12-14). The frantic lifestyle that seems so natural and enjoyable in carnal contexts can be a problem. That's why Paul tells Timothy to pray for government — not to assure sound fiscal policy or strengthen the military, but rather to provide circumstances conducive to "a tranquil and quiet life in all godliness and dignity" (1 Timothy 2:2). We could spend our days hiding from the government in caves, evangelizing at the peril of life and freedom. But it would be much easier if we did not have to.

There is something romantic about the idea of dying for our faith, suffering like the Lord and His apostles did. And it's easy to assume from the comfort of our relatively safe surroundings that we would pass the tests they passed. But our time and energy would be better spent making the most of the opportunities we have, rather than imagining circumstances that might not come to pass. We will have challenges aplenty, regardless of our time and conditions; truly, "Each day has enough trouble of its own" (Matthew 6:34).

The Chinese used to say, when they wanted to curse someone, "May you live in interesting times." Perhaps they were not too far wrong.

Further Reading

Matthew 6:25-34

Matthew 22:15-22

Philippians 4:4-7

What advantages do Christians in free societies enjoy? How might we take those advantages for granted?

_____

_____

_____

Doug says ...

When I got to substitute for the preacher a few Sundays ago, I didn't want to just do the same-old- same-old. So I made the case against putting children in drama, gymnastics, swimming, and bal-let. I knew some of our kids are in these activities. I was applying the principles the preacher empha-sized the week before. But instead of thanking me for my support, he has preached three sermons in a row on "love your neighbor" topics. Message received: Don't rock the boat.

What would you say to Doug?

_____

_____

_____

A Lesson from Your Bible—2 Kings 14:1-20

Amaziah assumed the throne in Jerusalem in a very challenging time. His father, Joash, was assassinated by political insurgents after he fell from the faith and killed Zechariah, the son of his mentor Jehoiada (2 Chronicles 24:20-27). But Amaziah did not overreact. He meted out justice to the killers without going overboard, as some might have. He established himself as a ruler who regarded God and God's law. And he met with early military success, winning a significant victory over Edom.

Having established peace in his nation and peace with his immediate enemies, though, Amaziah had the bit between his teeth. He sent word to Jehoash, who was ruling the northern tribes of Israel at the time, that he wanted to meet him in battle. Jehoash, not desiring a fight with his fellow Israelites, sent a message back to Amaziah containing a parable intended to teach Amaziah some humility:

"The thorn bush which was in Lebanon sent to the cedar which was in Lebanon, saying, 'Give your daughter to my son in marriage.' But there passed by a wild beast that was in Lebanon and trampled the thorn bush. You have indeed defeated Edom, and your heart has become proud. Enjoy your glory and stay at home; for why should you provoke trouble so that you, even you, would fall, and Judah with you?" (2 Kings 14:9-10)

Amaziah's pride kept him from taking Jehoash's good counsel, and he lost the battle. Not only that, but he was captured, and Jerusalem was sacked. Perhaps with this defeat in mind, Amaziah, like his father before him, was chased from the throne and assassinated by his people (2 Kings 14:18-19).

Amaziah's motives for going to war with Jehoash are not specified. It is safe to assume, though, that this fight with his people was easily avoidable. Perhaps the "thorn bush" should have been content with what he had instead of aspiring to something greater.

Why do brethren pick fights with one another? _____

_____

_____

A Lesson from Your Elder

Some people are just scrappers. They like to mix things up, make people uncomfortable. Usually, the rationale is getting people out of ruts or making them think for themselves. Usually, though, it's really about making the scrappers look and feel important. Trust me. Recovering scrapper talking here.

Fights come frequently enough without us inviting them. So let's not invite them.

I love you, and I'm praying for you.

> *O God and Father above,*
> *Please give us the peace that passes un-*
> *derstanding, both in our own hearts and*
> *between our brethren. Help us value it*
> *and preserve it, and only break it when we*
> *must do so to remain at peace with You.*
> *In Jesus' name,*
> *Amen.*

From *PLAIN TALK*

Stuff About Things

Someone has said, "Big people talk about ideas; mediocre people talk about things; and little people talk about people." Well, that's good enough to give us something to talk about, if we can measure up to it.

The word conversation as used in the KJ Bible meant "manner of life." We have both the early and later meaning of the term in mind when we say, the caliber of a man may be measured by his conversation; but we lean heavily toward the idea that his speech betrays the rest of him. Jesus said, "Out of the abundance of the heart the mouth speaketh." (Matt.12:34)

Big people talk about ideas. This is not to say they have no concern for their fellow-man, nor for everyday affairs of life; but they have learned to be objective. They are motivated by high ideals, and pattern their lives by noble principles. These require understanding, and translation into workable programs. They meditate on these ideas, talk about them with others, and study their application to past history and to the present. Perhaps they, are not so much interested in what happened, as to why. Their view is wide, hence they see themselves very small.

Mediocre people are bound in a maze of things. Cumbered about much serving; their's not to reason why, but to do, and die. I suppose the world owes much to the mediocre, but they exact a fearsome toll. Their vision limited to immediate circumstances, like sheep without a shepherd, they wander aimlessly. They are "too busy" building barns to contemplate the value of the soul. They find a measure of comfort in being "average" and criticize the climber because he rocks their boat. Here are the masses of "good" people who allow evil to triumph because they "Keep quiet," or talk about other things.

But little people just talk about people. Their world is purely personal, and everything and every body is measured by the effect upon oneself. There are no principles involved in their own thinking, hence, they can not imagine others standing up for principles. They have never felt compelled to act because of ideals, so they impugn the motives of others. Ask them who took the city of Jericho and they'll declare they didn't, and then say that you accused them of it.

Poor little dried up souls, with a big big debt to pay on judgement day.

From PLAIN TALK, August 1965, pg. 8

PROPER ROLES

"A woman must quietly receive instruction with entire submissiveness. But I do not allow a woman to teach or exercise authority over a man, but to remain quiet."

—1 Timothy 2:11-12

Virtually any human society has roles, by the very nature of things. Some are good at one thing, some another. Some have extra time, some have extra strength, and some have extra creativity. Everyone being alike would be counterproductive. Thankfully we have different roles in the church. The Holy Spirit made it so in the days of special gifts (Ephesians 4:7-12), and providence continues to make it so today. We should not waste time bickering over the nature of our respective roles — eyes wanting to be ears and such like (1 Corinthians 12:14-18). We should be busy serving as God has empowered us to serve.

It is important to emphasize, men are not given leadership in the church because we feel they are more suited to it; they are given leadership because God has determined that it should be so. He created Eve to assist Adam, not vice versa; additionally, Eve initially brought sin into the world by being deceived (1 Timothy 2:13-14). That is two rationalizations more than we need. If two are not enough, or if you do not find them compelling, then we should do things God's way for the first, most basic reason: because He is God, and we are not.

If we are granted the tranquility of life for which we should pray, the men of the church should feel free to be seen leading worship, "lifting up holy hands, without wrath and dissension" (1 Timothy 2:8). They assert themselves as spiritual leaders. Women, by contrast, behave "modestly and discreetly" (1 Timothy 2:9). Their godliness is seen through their submissiveness. Godliness has application to clothing choices, certainly; the main point, though, is to emphasize the role God has given women in the church — and the role He has not given them. By doing the things assigned to them — including matters withheld from men, such

Further Reading

1 Corinthians 12:13-21

Ephesians 4:7-16

1 Peter 3:1-9

as childbearing — they show themselves to be as much children of God as their husbands (1 Timothy 2:15).

Does Galatians 3:28 mean there is no distinction in roles between men and women in the church? If not, explain what it does mean?

_____

_____

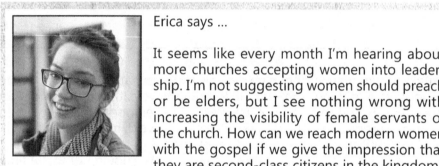

Erica says ...

It seems like every month I'm hearing about more churches accepting women into leadership. I'm not suggesting women should preach or be elders, but I see nothing wrong with increasing the visibility of female servants of the church. How can we reach modern women with the gospel if we give the impression that they are second-class citizens in the kingdom?

What would you say to Erica?

_____

_____

_____

A Lesson from Your Bible—Numbers 12

Moses holds a position in Israelite history like no other. Abraham was the father of the nation, and David brought the nation to prominence, but it was through Moses that Israel became a nation. Moses brought them out of bondage and gave them freedom. Moses gave them the Law that bears his name. Moses led them through the wilderness for 40 years, all the way to the edge of the Promised Land.

Strange, then, that his leadership should be questioned by, of all people, his own older brother and sister. Apparently, in reaction to Moses' marriage to a Cushite (a woman of whom we know nothing other than what we are told here), Aaron and Miriam asserted their authority. In Numbers 12:2, they say, "Has the LORD indeed spoken only through Moses? Has He not spoken through us as well?"

It is no accident that this is the context in which we are told of Moses' humility. Moses, who eventually chronicled this event for succeeding generations, did not want to appear as though he were threatened, or that he considered power to be hoarded to the detriment of others. He assumed the position of leader because God gave him that position. He was content to serve in that role, although it was not always easy or comfortable. Miriam and Aaron were not content and were chastened by God. Miriam herself was smitten with leprosy, temporarily quarantining her from the people and halting their march to Canaan for a week. Given that Aaron was not similarly punished, and that Miriam's name occurs before her brother's when the complaint is mentioned (Numbers 12:1), it well may be that the insurrection was Miriam's idea initially.

Democracy may be a fine thing in secular government, but in God's kingdom, we go where we are told to go and accept whatever capacity of service He places on us there. Failing to do so shows an egotistical attitude that has nothing to do with furthering His cause and everything to do with elevating our status. We only destroy ourselves and hurt His cause by claiming a role that is not ours to claim.

Is authority to be desired? If so, why and to what end? _____

_____

_____

A Lesson from Your Elder

We spend way too much time talking about what we are capable of doing, or what we would enjoy doing, or how much of an improvement we could bring to a particular task. This is not about you finding fulfillment. This is about being part of the body of Christ. And that means accepting the role given to you, both by the Lord and by the elders, and excelling in it.

Strive for the greater gifts, certainly, to take 1 Corinthians 12:31 a bit out of context. But first, learn to use the gifts you have, and find contentment in them. And remember, the biggest egotists in the world are those who think they are the best servants.

I love you, and I'm praying for you.

> O God and Father above,
> Thank you for the diversity of skills, works and opportunities in the body. Help these young ones build themselves up in the faith and the tools of the faith, training themselves for future service in the Kingdom. And while they work and wait, help them glorify You and elevate their brethren in their current circumstances.
> In Jesus' name,
> Amen.

From *PLAIN TALK*

Home, For The Grown-Ups

God made man, and woman. That is just about as basic as a study can get. And the next most basic step is, "Therefore shall a man leave his father and his mother, and shall cleave unto his wife, and they shall be one flesh" (Gen. 2:21-25). Jesus adds, "What therefore God hath joined together, let no man put asunder" (Matt. 19:6). The home is the most basic element in society.

We do not refer to mere biological procreation. Artificial insemination, state supervised harems, or temporary relationships may suffice for this. But in a home former ties and individual aspirations are second in importance to the preservation of this permanent unit. Its roles of trainer, protector and stabilizer far outweigh that of procreator. Women Libbers, socialized governments and current morals may minimize its importance, but revelation and historical evidence cry out against their error.

The "first division" of the Ten Commandments has to do with God. He is ONE, SPIRIT, HOLY, and the God of DELIVERANCE. But the "second division" has to do with man, and begins with the fifth command: "Honor thy father and thy mother..." The sixth command protects LIFE, and the seventh protects the sanctity of the HOME: Thou shalt not commit adultery" (Ex. 20:1). Further reference to the inviolable nature of the home is found in the last command: "Thou shalt not covet thy neighbor's house, wife, etc." Paul pictures Christ's love for His people in terms of the home, not as a "party" loyalty (Eph. 5:23-f); for we are the "family" of God (3:14-f). Reader's Digest (Mar. 78, p.111 quotes Michael Novak, Harper's Magazine, as saying, "The family is the critical center of social force. It is a seedbed of economic skills and attitudes toward work. It is a stronger agency of educational success than the school and a stronger teacher of the religious imagination than the church. Political and social planning in a wise social order begins with the axiom: What strengthens the family strengthens society."

What Novak calls "religious imagination" I would call "faith;" but I would have to agree that the role of the home is greater in this field than is "the church" — for I assume he refers to collective activity, in a "church building," under institutional guidance. Many people, including many brethren, have never learned that God's family (the "church") also acts distributively, as saints function in domestic, economic and civic affairs. It is absurd to think that Bible classes and an hour or so of formal "worship" can have a greater influence upon society than can a truly "Christian" home.

And I'm going to say this if it cancels half our readers. By "Christian home" I do NOT refer to one that simply transfers formal worship or "class" activities from the church building into "daily devotionals," puts "God Is Love" on the wall, and formally expresses "thanks" for the food. These worthwhile endeavors may even have an adverse effect upon our children unless they are coupled with a genuine atmosphere of fairness, understanding, love and faith in God.

From PLAIN TALK, June 1978, pg. 8

LEADERSHIP

"It is a trustworthy statement: if any man aspires to the office of overseer, it is a fine work he desires to do."

— 1 Timothy 3:1

Presumably, Paul had appointed the first group of elders in Ephesus. It would seem that the process needed to be repeated — or at the very least, Paul expected that it would need to take place in the near future. Or perhaps he expected Timothy himself to serve as an elder at some point. (Timothy seems to have been in his mid to late 30s at the time of this writing.) The need to appoint elders prompted the Holy Spirit to send through Paul's pen a description of the right sort of man to oversee the work of a local church.

Often the traits listed in 1 Timothy 3:2-7 and in Titus 1:5-9 are called "qualifications." When a man can check off that he posseses these "qualifications," it implies he is qualified to serve as an elder. But would this not indicate that an elder in Crete, where Titus was, would not have to be gentle (a qualification missing from the list in Titus 1)? Or that elders in Ephesus need not be sensible or just (qualifications missing from the list in 1 Timothy 3)? Or that no elders should have brotherly love, a trait omitted in both lists?

A better way of looking at these traits is that they form a composite sketch of a certain kind of man — and yes, he must be a man. Both lists describe a seasoned Christian, full of the fruit of the Spirit, disciplined in his lifestyle, and sound in his faith. A man who fits either description is a proper candidate for consideration.

Timothy is also given a list of traits for deacons, another office in the church (Philippians 1:1). The specific roles of these "servants" are not designated; it may be similar to the work given to the seven appointed men in Acts 6:1-6. In any event, they should be "tested" before being given this special role. Although elders are not mentioned as being "tested," such can be implied through the listed traits; the most obvious way, though hardly the only way, for an elder to be tested, and the way truest to the context, would be for them to serve as deacons.

Further Reading

Titus 1:5-9

Acts 6:1-6

1 Peter 5:1-5

The "women" in 1 Timothy 3:11 are attached to the deacons in the context; it seems most likely they refer to the deacons' wives. As is the case with the male roles, the description could be neatly summed up as, "Be the best Christian you can be in the position you find yourself."
Leadership is "a fine work." But it is work.

Can women be "servants" of the church? If so, is this in harmony with the principle of male leadership?

_____

_____

_____

Doug says ...

I understand about submitting to elders. But what if the elders are wrong? Their way may have been appropriate a decade or three ago, but Christians today, especially young Christians, get very frustrated with the ruts that have been dug for us. We need new approaches. The old ways aren't sinful, exactly, but isn't it wrong to not give God our best? And this isn't anywhere near our best. I tried to explain that to them, but they wouldn't listen. Now, what am I supposed to do?

What would you say to Doug?

_____

_____

_____

A Lesson from Your Bible—Numbers 16

If you start reading in Numbers 16, you miss the irony of the whole Korah story. It is placed in the text just a page or two after the story of how Moses took the people to the Promised Land. He sent spies into the land, at God's instruction (Numbers 13:2), so the people would know what God was giving them. But 10 of the 12 spies convinced the entire nation that the land was unattainable, and they began making preparations for choosing a new leader who would take them back to Egypt (Numbers 14:1-4). God cursed that generation, dooming them to wander in the wilderness instead of entering Canaan (Numbers 14:28-29).

This is the nation Korah insisted was "holy, every one of them" in Numbers 16:3. Korah and his followers said Moses had assumed too much power for himself. This Moses was the same man, remember, who begged God not to destroy the nation and build another one from Moses' own seed (Numbers 14:11-19) — for the second time (Exodus 32:9-14). Strange behavior for a megalomaniac.

Regardless of how Korah felt the government of the people should work, God had already established, implemented and announced His plan. To ask for or even demand an alteration was nothing less than rebellion against Moses — and more than that, rebellion against God. Korah and his company were swallowed up by the earth the next day, 250 of them in all. Sadly, the people blamed Moses and Aaron, prompting God to strike the people again and prompting Moses and Aaron to intercede for them again (Numbers 16:41-50).

What traits of elders do you see working in Moses and Aaron in this story?

_____

_____

_____

A Lesson from Your Elder

I love the passion and energy of young people. But just as oldsters like me need a jolt of energy sometimes, so also the youngsters need restraint. It may seem to young people that leadership moves impossibly and impractically slowly. But patience is a virtue. Slow is often safer than quick.

Remember, the oldsters were youngsters too, long ago, and lived to tell the tale. It may be that they are trying to help you avoid making the mistakes they made.

I love you, and I'm praying for you.

> O God and Father above,
> Thank you for the wisdom that age and
> experience bring, and for the guidance
> You provide in the local church through
> elders. Give them wisdom to guide, and
> give the young ones wisdom to follow —
> and to learn, so that one day they too may
> guide.
> In Jesus' name,
> Amen.

From *PLAIN TALK*

Going After The Candy

A doting parent wished to demonstrate to a visitor the willingly obedient nature of his son. Calling the boy, he gave him a dime and then commanded (?) "Son, go buy yourself some candy!" Without a word of dissent, the boy obeyed.

If the boy would show a martyr's complex and brag to his friends about how well he obeyed his father, this might be a good illustration of the way some church members act.

In Col. 2:20-23 Paul speaks of subjection to man-made ordinances as "will-worship" -- something obviously unacceptable to God. This "voluntary humility" (vs. 18) was of no value in the service of God (in that it showed no true subjection to Christ, the Head; vs. 19) and did not contribute to the control of fleshly desires -- in that it was, in reality, the satisfaction of morbid self-indulgence. (Read carefully vs. 18-23, ARV)

Certain pagan worshipers lie on beds of nails, or cut themselves with knives, in the misguided belief that this pleases God. Their suffering is in vain, being wholly unauthorized.

Certain Jewish worshipers in the time of Christ disfigured their faces so that their "fasting" would appear unto men. Jesus called them "hypocrites." (Matt. 6:16-f) Their misery was self-inflicted, for self-satisfaction -- a "going after the candy" -- and hence no true service to God.

ASH WEDNESDAY AND FISH

Now men have decreed that "Lenten" seasons should be observed, begun by a ceremonial daubing of ashes upon the forehead. Mardi Gras celebrants must sober up with coffee, fish takes the place of beef, and even little children must "give up" something—like chewing gum.

And what business of mine is it?? Exactly the same business that was Paul's. (Col. 2:l8-23) (The transfer is indicated in 2 Tim. 2:1-2)

Many wonderful people are deceived by human traditions, and make heavy personal sacrifices in the belief that they thus serve the Lord. This "will-worship" is in vain. The greatest sacrifice they could make, and the only truly productive sacrifice would be to give themselves to Christ for service according to His word.

From PLAIN TALK, March 1965, pg. 8

DISCIPLINE

"But have nothing to do with worldly fables fit only for old women. On the other hand, discipline yourself for the purpose of godliness."

— 1 Timothy 4:7

You may be on a diet. Or perhaps you have a regular exercise regimen. Maybe it is something as simple as an inflexible time for getting out of bed. The older we are the more inclined we are to set strict rules for ourselves. Having set rules is ironic for those who have recently passed the point where parents were setting those strict rules. Discipline, we come to understand, is a useful thing. More than that, it is often a necessary thing.

But it is not a natural thing. Left to ourselves, apart from any sense of accountability, we likely will slide into comfortable ruts in which we ask little from ourselves. An honest appraisal, however, will show us how that sort of attitude will keep us from growing — and may even hurt us in the short term.

Discipline for godliness is very much the same. It may be easier for us to listen to "worldly fables" for advice as to how to serve God in this life. Philosophers who may claim to be "Bible-based" may tell us to follow their rules or to make up our own. There is little to be gained for them in making life more difficult than God makes it. But we did not agree to follow Jesus because it was going to be easy, but rather because He is Lord. Therefore whether God's expectations are "easy" or "hard" has nothing to do with it. We work. And if that is difficult, we work harder.

Depending on your translation, Paul tells Timothy that physical exercise profits "a little" or "little." Is he saying that it is good, but just not as good as spiritual discipline? Or is he completely diminishing its importance entirely? Either way, we should be disciplined enough in our exercise of faith that we can turn away from the temptation of sin as easily as we can stay an extra five minutes on an exercise bike.

Further Reading

Proverbs
24:30-34

1 Corinthians
9:19-27

Hebrews 12:4-13

What is the part of serving the Lord that requires the most discipline?

_____

_____

_____

Doug says ...

My schedule keeps me from being as regular in my attendance as I would like to be. I have school, plus I am working. Free time is tough to find. Jesus comes first, certainly. I always make sure to be present to take the Lord's Supper, and I read my Bible every night before bed. Right now I don't have much more to give than that. I am looking forward to the time when things lighten up a bit.

What would you say to Doug?

_____

_____

_____

A Lesson from Your Bible—1 Kings 13

When Jeroboam rebelled against the authority of the house of David, he took ten of the tribes with him. The resulting nation, the northern kingdom of "Israel," soon drifted further and further from God's plan, eventually resulting in the nation's destruction at the hands of the Assyrian empire.

It began when Jeroboam made golden calves to serve as substitutes for proper Jehovah worship in Jerusalem. A prophet from Judah came to Jeroboam's idolatrous ceremony in Bethel and condemned him, causing the king's hand to wither. After the prophet asked God to restore Jeroboam's hand, Jeroboam offered the prophet rest and refreshment. The prophet refused, saying God had specifically prohibited him from eating or drinking during his stay in Bethel.

On his way home, the prophet encountered an older prophet. For reasons undisclosed to us, he took it upon himself to refresh the young prophet at his house, even saying God had directed him to do so. The young prophet believed him and accepted his bread and water. At dinner God spoke to him, saying he had disobeyed and that he would not be brought back to be buried with his fathers. True to his word, God sent a lion to attack and kill the young prophet on the road, and the older prophet retrieved the body and buried it in the grave he had reserved for himself, and in which he eventually would be buried as well.

God's expectations of us are not always simple. They may not fit in with our plans or our agenda. They may not make much sense to our human minds. But then, that's why we are told to "walk by faith, not by sight" (2 Corinthians 5:7). We have to accept God's rules without question, simply because they are God's rules. And we must brace ourselves for Satan's on-slaught. Inevitably, we will be given an opportunity to break the rules. We will have ample excuses. We may even have righteous souls encouraging us in our rebellion. But we must remain strong. If we fail, as the young prophet did, we face the wrath of God — and, potentially, eternal consequences. "But we are not of those who shrink back to destruction, but of those who have faith to the preserving of the soul" (Hebrews 10:39).

Can temptations that come through brethren be tougher to withstand than temptations from the world? Explain and provide examples. _____

_____

_____

A Lesson from Your Elder

It's easy to assume when you are young that the hard work can wait until tomorrow, that you can afford to give less than your best right now because less will be expected later—and besides, you have plenty of time to catch up. But bad habits can form quickly. There's never a time like the present to develop good ones instead.

You can't be a disciple without discipline. So start being a disciple now.

I love you, and I'm praying for you.

> *O God and Father above,*
> *Thank you for hardship, and the discipline*
> *it brings. Thank you for making our lives*
> *difficult. Let challenges work endurance in*
> *the lives of these young people, so they*
> *will be able to be examples to others in*
> *the challenges that are still to come for*
> *them.*
> *In Jesus' name,*
> *Amen.*

From PLAIN TALK

Here's a new look at ulcers: For years my doctors have been telling me to "slow down," "mustn't let things bother you," "those problems will be here when you are gone," "take more vacations," etc. I think I got my ulcers over an internal battle with my conscience, brought on by too much relaxing. But I could always say I was following doctor's orders-- until some smart aleck up at Scott-White Clinic said he thought the world had benefited most by the concerned, the "got to do something about it" guys; and where would we be if somebody did not have back trouble, break-downs or ulcers in the effort to change the course of human events.

The good doctor might just have something there. Suppose everyone decided to "take it easy." It's hard enough now to find a place to hunt that is not full of red-shirted relaxers.

A student once reported to the professor (I believe it was Agassiz) that he did not have his theme prepared because he had not felt well. The Swiss naturalist replied that few great things would ever be accomplished if they could be done only by those who "felt well." People who do great things, do them against odds.

They can't sleep for thinking about the needs and ways of overcoming the problems. They give themselves, maybe they "burn out," but their kind have a tremendous effect upon the world.

We are not put in this world to "relax"; we are here to accomplish, to serve as faithful stewards, and to glorify God. As the editor of the Gospel Guardian, in a splendid editorial 12-14-67 said, "It is certainly true that, expressed or unexpressed, realized or unrealized, the 'sense of mission' dominates every life that is worth the living." Again, "Life is a trust, a stewardship, a sacred commitment. Man is not free 'to live his own life,' for his life is not his own; he has been 'bought with a price.'"

An exaggerated sense of importance may turn a man's head; and pride is so prevalent we must wave a warning. But genuine "total commitment" and a "sense of mission" do not produce selfish, egocentric pride, nor is one's "mission" served by such. It is only by forgetting one's self that we can begin to sense a real purpose here; and trade the harsh competitive struggle for a "place among people" for the more meaningful battle against error, and a place with God.

From PLAIN TALK, January 1968, pg. 8

BEING AN EXAMPLE

"Let no one look down on your youthfulness, but rather in speech, conduct, love, faith and purity, show yourself an example of those who believe."
— 1 Timothy 4:12

You are an example. You may not be trying to be one. You may not realize you are one. But you are.

You could be an example of unbelief, like the Israelites of old. We read Paul's breakdown of Israel's rebellion in the wilderness in 1 Corinthians 10:1-12, which concludes with the admonition, "Therefore let him who thinks he stands take heed that he does not fall." We, too, can be idolatrous or immoral. We, too, can put God to the test. We, too, can grumble. And if we think simply being a child of God is sufficient, we should think of what happened to that generation of God's children. They were doomed to wander in the wilderness for 40 years, just short of the Promised Land. Thus they not only are examples of unbelief, but they also serve as examples of God's wrath against His people who prove to be unworthy of His favor.

On the other hand, you can be an example of faith. By imitating Jesus' example of love, service, and obedience, you can show the impact He is having on your life. Perhaps by doing so, succeeding generations will be able to look back at your life for strength and courage as we look back at Abraham, Isaac, Jacob, and the other worthies named in Hebrews 11 and throughout the rest of the Bible.

You will never be perfect. However, you can have the perfect attitude to which Paul refers in Philippians 3:15-16 — the attitude that strives toward the mark of the one perfect Example. If you do that and persevere, in the end, you can have enough confidence to say with Paul, "Be imitators of me, just as I also am of Christ" (1 Corinthians 11:1).

Further Reading

1 Corinthians 10:1-12

Hebrews 11:8-16

John 13:1-16

What are some areas in which any Christian can be a good example? _____

_____

Erica says ...

An example of what? I have nothing of substance to add to the discussion in our public Bible classes. I don't have any great life experiences from which to draw. I don't have any remarkable skills — certainly nothing that could be used for the church. I am trying my best to be a Christian, but I don't see that my "light" is powerful enough to make a real difference.

What would you say to Erica?

_____

_____

_____

A Lesson from Your Bible—Joshua 1

Joshua was not a young man when he assumed the mantle of leadership from Moses. Nor was he inexperienced; he had served at Moses' right hand through the 40 years in the wilderness. He had seen Moses' courage every day, and on at least one occasion he had the opportunity to show his courage by leading the people in battle (Exodus 17:8-13). One would think he would have been remarkably well positioned to take the people into the Promised Land. And yet God saw fit to tell Joshua to "be strong and courageous" (or words to that immediate effect) three times in the first nine verses of the book that bears Joshua's name.

God reminded Joshua that He had made promises and that He intended to keep them. He assured him that his enemies would not be able to stand before him. But still, Joshua would be responsible for obeying the law given to him and the people by Moses. "This book of the law shall not depart from your mouth, but you shall meditate on it day and night so that you may be careful to do according to all that is written in it; for then you will make your way prosperous, and then you will have success" (Joshua 1:8).

God knew the people would be overwhelmed by the loss of Moses; they mourned him for 30 days (Deuteronomy 34:8). If their new leader was to be effective, he had to inspire confidence in them. And that confidence was to come only through God's word. By letting it direct his behavior, and particularly his speech, he would be emboldened to know God was blessing his activities. And when the people saw Joshua acting with the spirit of

Moses, serving the same God he served and with the same passion, they would be emboldened as well.

"Be strong and courageous." It is a command, not a suggestion. Failure to do so is to suggest that we doubt God. After all, how could we possibly lose heart if we believe God is fighting for us?

What are situations when we find our spiritual strength lagging? What can we do to renew it?

_____

_____

_____

A Lesson from Your Elder

Some of you have younger siblings. Those who do have almost certainly been told numerous times by your parents to be a good example for them. Usually, that means you should be polite, obedient, respectful, honest, and a host of other adjectives — all of which reflect not just a decent character, but also a character that is being shaped by God's word.

"I didn't ask for this," you may have said from time to time when being an example meant a sacrifice of some sort. But still, it is yours. Instead of chafing at it, embrace it. See it as part of the important role you have in the kingdom — not just in the future, but right here and right now.

I love you, and I'm praying for you.

> *O God and Father above,*
> *Thank you for the wonderful example that*
> *is being set by godly young people, both*
> *for those who are younger and for those*
> *who are older. Help them not grow weary*
> *in well doing, but rather press on to even*
> *greater examples of Christian virtue.*
> *In Jesus' name,*
> *Amen.*

From PLAIN TALK

He Never Let On!

The musical Oklahoma has a character. Judd, who is eulogized in a mock funeral as one who was kind and gentle and loved the whole human race. Only they never knowed it — he never let on.

Poor Judd is not dead — he isn't even sick. There are thousands of his kind in the church. They love all people and long to see the whole world converted — only the world never discovers this burning desire. They never let on, even to a hairdresser.

They love the truth, according to public prayers and songs. But if they attend Bible study at all, it is to give their opinion or experience, not to study the text. If a passage seems to run counter to their traditional concepts, they ignore it or explain it away.

They believe in salvation by grace — and if you push them hard enough, they will admit it. They know that one may fall from grace — i.e., someone other than themselves. If they really believe that the Lord will reveal and judge the secrets of their lives and thoughts, they never let on. You would never guess it. They love the brotherhood if not the brethren. They long for unity of all saints and would do almost anything to see all issues properly settled — except meeting with those with whom they differ for an honorable and scriptural discussion of the issues which divide them.

This is not intended as a blanket indictment of all church members, for I know the salt of the earth is at work. Christians are concerned and endeavor to teach their neighbors. Gospel preachers are demonstrating by sacrificial efforts their love for souls. There are those who care more for peace with God, than for approval of the party.

But this is a reminder that such love, concern, and endeavor are not done in a corner. If people about you have never suspected that you are a Christian, there's a good chance that you have never let on with a fair sample of Christian living. Do not ask me to preach your funeral.

From PLAIN TALK, October 1968, pg. 1

RESPECT

"Do not sharply rebuke an older man, but rather appeal to him as a father, to the younger men as brothers, the older women as mothers, and the younger women as sisters, in all purity."

— 1 Timothy 5:1-2

Back in my day, a comedian named Rodney Dangerfield made an entire career out of telling jokes about how he never got any respect. Not from his wife, not from his friends, not from his neighbors. Respect is generally something that we seek for ourselves. But the Bible spends far more time discussing the respect we give to others. We are sometimes told we have to give respect in order to receive it, and often that is true; but that is not why we respect others. We respect others because they are made in the image of God, just as we are. They deserve to be treated with dignity whether we receive it or not.

Earlier in the epistle, Paul noted that an overseer of the Lord's church required experience — in the family, in the church, and in the world. We usually call them "elders," after all. Such ones have earned our regard simply because of their years. That does not mean they are always right; in fact, they are to be condemned like anyone else "on the basis of two or three witnesses" (1 Timothy 5:19). But age certainly should not carry with it a connotation of irrelevance or incompetence. Often the haste that youth employs in pursuit of righteousness bypasses older and slower ones whose wisdom is sorely needed.

The "purity" we should show in our dealings with brethren is more than just sexual purity, although certainly, that is a part. We must be pure in our motives — serving the Lord and our brethren, not ourselves. It is easy to convince ourselves that our arrogance is rooted in righteousness. But God may be a harsher, more honest Judge.

Further Reading

Proverbs
4:1-12
10:1
16:31

We feel the need to be important. But our real need is wisdom. And wisdom comes far more easily when we listen than when we talk.

Do we "owe" it to the church to be leaders? Why or why not? _____

_____

_____

Doug says ...

I've heard all the arguments against social drinking. Bottom line, Paul told Timothy to "use a little wine." And he said it in the context of being free from sin. The elders are always warning us about what "the first step" might lead to, but that doesn't mean the first step is wrong in and of itself. We can all agree that drunkenness is wrong. But if Timothy could drink a little wine, why can't I?

What would you say to Doug?

_____

_____

_____

A Lesson from Your Bible—1 Kings 12:1-25

The kingdom passed with a bit of controversy when David died; Solomon eventually was installed on the throne after a failed coup attempt by his older brother, Adonijah. The transfer seemed to be set up to go much more smoothly upon Solomon's death. However, Rehoboam lacked the wisdom of his father — likely because, unlike Solomon, he did not ask God for it.

Instead, Rehoboam listened to his fellow human beings concerning how he should rule. And, as is always the case, he got some good advice and some not-so-good advice. His father's advisers (and note, even Solomon had advisers) told him to win the hearts of the people with kindness. His contemporaries, though, told him to impose his will on the people in as harsh a manner as might be managed. He should act like a bigger man than his father to gain more respect than his father.

It turns out people don't like to be pushed around. They don't like their taxes raised. They don't like to be told the coming days are going to be more painful than the days that are already passed. And so, true to God's promise to Jeroboam, most of the nation left the legacy of David and embarked on a legacy of selfishness and rebellion.

Most decisions in our lives are ultimately of no consequence. But some represent crossroads. Rehoboam had the opportunity to choose between service and pride, and he chose pride. He had the opportunity to choose between experience and familiarity, and he chose familiarity. He wound up spending the rest of his life dealing with the consequences of these bad choices, and so did the rest of the nation.

Since this was a fulfillment of prophecy (1 Kings 11:29-37), Rehoboam's failure fit into the plan of God for Israel. But just because God can work His will through our mistakes doesn't mean our mistakes are irrelevant, or that people will not suffer from them. It is lazy to rationalize our bad decisions by thinking, "Maybe good will come from this." The most obvious "good" result and perhaps the most important is that we recognize the consequences of bad decisions and commit to making better ones in the future.

What is the best advice you have ever received from an older person? Did you keep it or ignore it?

_____

_____

_____

A Lesson from Your Elder

Listening to old people is boring. The younger you are, the truer that statement becomes. But there are worse things than boredom. Ignorance, for instance. Or self-destruction. Granted, most of what they tell you will be useless. But not all of it. And just putting the time in will build in you respect for the aged that is valuable in and of itself.

Spend some time with an older person this week. Listen to their stories. You never know what nugget of wisdom you may find there.

I love you, and I'm praying for you.

> *O God and Father above,*
> *Thank you for every generation of Christians — young, old, and in between. Help us respect one another as we should, as befits creatures made in Your image and remade again in the image of Your Son.*
> *In Jesus' name,*
> *Amen.*

From *PLAIN TALK*

Stuff About Things

A soldier boy (from corn country) told a certain west-coast preacher: "I like your preaching better than any preaching I ever heered."

So pleased he couldn't let well enough alone, the preacher pressed for details. "Just what was it about my preaching that you liked?"

"Well," the boy replied, "I don't like no preaching a'tall, but your preaching is the nearest to my kind of preaching I ever heered." Now it's enough to give a feller the thumps.

I suppose everyone gets "taken down a notch" now and then, but vanity makes the fall a hard one. There are plenty of vain preachers; stuffed toads who think their pronouncements are treasured like jewels of a Maharaja. If they have an ounce of sense, they will not ask the members what they preached last Lord's Day.

But vanity doesn't stop with the preachers. The "know it all" doctor, the "don't cross me" judge, the small town beauty queen, the lineman who thinks he is an electrical genius -- most folks know the type and laugh up their sleeves at their antics. Maybe in our Walter Mitty moments, we all have a touch of this heady spirit and imagine we are something special. We get carried away with our dreams and begin to see ourselves as we somehow intended to be.

Dreams are necessary for advancement; and pity the man who has lost his self-respect -- who sees himself as utterly worthless. He likely will be. But he must have something more than vain (empty) dreams for a foundation. Ah yes, and building that real foundation will cure vanity.

Put the "know it all" to work, in a pond big enough to test his powers. Challenge his knowledge with the vast unknown, and let him seek his place among giants. If he will really study his field, quit fooling around on the surface and reach for the depths, he will begin to deflate. When he does not know and knows he does not know, he is a student. Teach him.

The rest of the proverb is interesting. If he knows and does not know he knows, he is asleep. Awaken him.

But there is more. If he does not know and does not know he does not know, he is a fool. Avoid him.

From PLAIN TALK, April 1967, pg. 8

RESPONSIBILITY

"But if anyone does not provide for his own, and especially for those of his household, he has denied the faith and is worse than an unbeliever."

— 1 Timothy 5:8

It makes you wonder what people mean exactly when they talk about responsibility.

We have responsibilities in this life. Parents are responsible for their children. When the time comes, those children are responsible for their parents. More than anything else, though, each of us is responsible for himself. Certainly we are blessed to have people who will help us bear our burdens in times of hardship (Galatians 6:2), and there is nothing wrong with availing ourselves of those relationships. However, depending upon others can become a crutch. We can become so dependent upon the actions of others that we forego reasonable actions on our behalf. That is not only lazy, but it also denies the work of God in us that is compelling us to put others before ourselves (Ephesians 5:28).

Children are dependent upon their parents by nature. As they grow, though, they assume more and more responsibility for their care and upkeep. They crave responsibility long before they are capable of properly exercising it. But trial and error help them grow into responsible adults in due time.

Depending on the church is much like depending on parents. It may be necessary for a time, but the goal is to be self-sufficient — not for reasons of pride or arrogance but to cease to be a burden to others. Only certain ones were permitted by Paul to be supported at all — essentially those who could not be supported any other way. Family responsibility was never to be superseded by the church. Asking the church to assume individual responsibilities is tantamount to subsidizing laziness and disrespect.

Further Reading

Galatians 6:1-5

Ephesians 6:1-4

Why does Paul emphasize the holiness and good works of "widows indeed?"

_____

_____

Erica says ...

I have been feeling bad about not being more involved with the church, so I asked the elders about perhaps teaching the little kids' class. They referred me to the appropriate deacon, who said he would think about it. That was two months ago. Now he says maybe I could "assist" one of the older ladies as they teach. Apparently, I'm not a good enough Christian to teach a 3-year-old.

What would you say to Erica?

_____

_____

_____

A Lesson from Your Bible—1 Samuel 2 - 4

Eli was a good man and a good mentor to his young ward, Samuel. He judged Israel 40 years (1 Samuel 4:18), and there is no indication he was to be blamed in so doing — except in one respect. He put his sons in positions of authority when he knew they were unworthy, and he left them there when they refused to change (1 Samuel 2:12-17). He made at least token efforts to chasten them (1 Samuel 2:22-25), but they refused to listen.

Eventually, a man of God spoke to Eli and condemned him and the rest of the Levites for using their office to make themselves fat and honor their sons above Him (1 Samuel 2:27-29). Although Eli condemned some of his sons' actions, he seemed willing to profit from them as well. The context of Eli's treatment of his sons certainly indicates that Eli himself was guilty of prioritizing his sons' short-term welfare over the glory of the God he was supposed to be serving.

As a result, the entire Levitic system of worship was going to be disrupted. A "faithful priest" (obviously Samuel) would serve Him properly, and the remnants of Eli's house would be left to beg for a meager service position simply to eat — and Hophni and Phineas, the wicked sons of Eli, would die in a single day (1 Samuel 2:34-36).

Eli was left in charge of the house of God, and he was unfaithful in that duty. God held him responsible for that. He could have pointed to his good intentions or his noble sentiments. He could have claimed his "boys" were grown men and responsible for their actions — which they were. But clearly, God did not think that was enough.

The charge is given to us today as a "holy priesthood" (1 Peter 2:4-5) should cause us to review the story of Eli carefully. Certainly we "do our job" to the best of our ability. But when we have others in our charge, we must make sure they serve properly as well. Their attitude, good or bad, reflects on us. And for those in charge of others (some to parents, all to church elders), we must make sure we do nothing to tarnish their name — let alone the name of the Savior.

What can or should parents do to chasten grown children?

_____

_____

_____

A Lesson from Your Elder

None of us parents understood into what we were getting. But we got into it anyway, and we're making the best of it. Our "best" isn't always that good. But we take the job seriously, even if we don't always act accordingly.

You need to learn to take your responsibilities seriously as well. You don't have as many as your parents now, but you will. And in the meantime, please bear with your parents as you are growing into your new role. You wear their name. Your actions and inactions reflect on them — as well as on the Savior whose name you wear.

I love you, and I'm praying for you.

> *O God and Father above,*
> *Please give us patience with ourselves and*
> *with others as we grow into the roles You*
> *have given us, and as those roles change.*
> *But do not let us be satisfied. Help us*
> *know our jobs, do it well, and encourage*
> *others in doing the same.*
> *In Jesus' name,*
> *Amen.*

From *PLAIN TALK*

It's Me. O Lord!

A recent class in Personal Work, (defined, Individual interest in the souls of others;) was asked: "What do you consider to be the greatest hindrance to successful personal work?"

With variation, but without exception, the members of the class replied, "Indifference on our part!"

Of course, there were other hindrances: a feeling of inadequacy, negative response in the past, general lack of interest in religion among people caught up in the affairs of this life, etc. But everyone agreed that the big problem is close to home. "Not my brother, not my sister, but it's me O Lord; Standing in the need of prayer!"

An Arkansas farmer once jokingly told a dinner guest: "I ain't got no table manners, and don't never pass nothing. You'll just have to make out the best you can." He was somewhat jolted when the guest replied, "If you know you aren't acting right, why don't you try to do better?"

That is a low blow, isn't it? Have we need for such a jolt respecting our relation toward God? Have we come to the point that we can boldly acknowledge our weakness -- maybe even make a joke of it -- and go our way feeling that penance is complete? Jesus' classic example of repentance (Matt. 21:28-f) says, "but afterward he repented, and went." AND WENT! What credit is one due, who recognizes his sins but refuses to do anything about it? The sin is compounded. "To him that knoweth to do good, and doeth it not, to him it is sin." (Jas. 4:17) "For if we sin willfully after that we have received the knowledge of the truth, there remaineth no more sacrifice for sins, but a certain fearful looking for of judgment and fiery indignation, which shall devour the adversaries." (Heb. 10:26-27)

I know literally dozens of people who excuse themselves on the basis that "everybody does it" or "I don't want to be a hypocrite." Yet they are highly incensed if one accepts their self-confessed sinner status, and warns them of the wrath to come. IT'S TIME WE QUIT ACTING LIKE CHILDREN!!

From PLAIN TALK, September 1967, pg. 1

CONTROVERSY

"...he is conceited and understands nothing; but he has a morbid interest in controversial questions and disputes about words, out of which arise envy, strife, abusive language, evil suspicions, and constant friction between men of depraved mind..."

— 1 Timothy 6:3-5

At various times in my life—and, judging from Paul's letters, going all the way back to the First Century—there have been Christians, particularly preachers, who have tried to make themselves look important by being "experts" in some technical point of the gospel. I do not mean to imply that every issue of controversy is, by its nature, irrelevant; everything in the gospel is controversial to someone. But some issues have no practical relevance for our lives. Often they deal with "filling the holes" in the record regarding matters in which God's entire process is not revealed. (Has it occurred to anyone that we mere mortals may not be able to comprehend the deep things of God fully?)

You can easily become the house expert on the history of bananas, or the presidency of Millard Fillmore, or Guamanian architecture. You have to study more than anyone else—and generally, that's not difficult. It works the same way with arcane Bible topics such as the origin of Satan, the baptism of John and the exact timing of the Lord's return. Gaining and demonstrating expertise in such matters does little for the cause of Christ; mostly it is an exercise in ego. Additionally, it creates opportunity for equally egotistical ones on opposite sides to disagree, and perhaps even splinter the fellowship of saints.

Factiousness among the people of God will occur enough on its own (1 Corinthians 1:10-17). In points of doctrine, it can even serve to separate the faithful from the pretenders (1 Corinthians 11:17-21). But when its only cause is personal pride and ambition, we would do well to stamp it out.

How do we know which issues are worth fighting?

Further Reading

Philippians 3:2-7

James 3:13-18

_____

_____

_____

Doug says ...

I don't understand why we keep discussing matters that have split brethren in past decades and centuries. Surely what brings us together in Christ is more important than what drives us apart, right? I don't want to spend precious energy and time deciding whose side I'm on in the latest brotherhood brawl. I'm with Jesus; I think that's all that matters.

What would you say to Doug?

_____

_____

_____

A Lesson from Your Bible—3 John 9-12

We don't know anything about the church where Gaius was — its location, its size, whether Gaius was a preacher or elder, etc. We know little more about Gaius himself; scholars are indeterminate as to whether he matches one or more of several men by that name mentioned in the New Testament. All we know about the situation regarding John's third epistle is what he wrote in that epistle — and that isn't much.

John appears to be confident in Gaius, a lover of truth, to be able to persuade the brethren there to reject the leadership of Diotrephes and accept the example of Demetrius instead. Diotrephes had taken it upon himself to not only reject the inspired words of John and perhaps others, but he had also made attempts (perhaps successful ones) to exclude from the church those who stood against him. The easiest way to win an argument has always been to quash dissent. And unfortunately, this approach is often successful in churches. Christians tend by their nature to be non-confrontational and humble, and they give the benefit of the doubt to brethren when their motives are being questioned. However, controversy arises from time to time. On that day, it is far more important that we choose the right side rather than feeling good about the current leadership.

Demetrius, who seems to have been a stalwart in the church whom Diotrephes had not been able to marginalize, was the one worthy of imitation. He stood steadfast in favor of apostolic authority, and it appears he was not ashamed to be seen doing so. A church full of such ones will give the Diotrepheses of the church nothing with which to work.

Pray for peace in the church, certainly. But true wisdom is pure first, then peaceable (James 3:17). Standing for truth in time of war is far better than surrendering truth to make peace.

In what ways might the spirit of Diotrephes arise in churches today?

_____

_____

_____

A Lesson from Your Elder

The secret to success, someone once suggested, is first to create a need, then fill it. It's a tried and true formula. But our idea of success and the Lord's idea are rarely the same. That's certainly the case with our efforts to be "important" in the church.

Becoming the loudest — and, in our minds at least, the most intelligent — voice in the room is a good way to attract attention, and perhaps a following. But we already have a Leader. What we need are better followers.

If our real objective is to make ourselves look bigger than our brethren, we can pretty much rest assured it's a bad objective. Back up and reassess.

I love you, and I'm praying for you.

> *O God and Father above,*
> *We ask that these young people be grant-*
> *ed a measure of peace, in the church if*
> *not in the world. But if their lot should be*
> *war and not peace, let them be warriors*
> *for You and not for their manufactured*
> *causes. Help love rule over all — love for*
> *You, love for our brethren, and love for the*
> *work You have assigned to us.*
> *In Jesus' name,*
> *Amen.*

From PLAIN TALK

"Study to be Quiet"

Paul wrote the Thessalonians that they should study to be quiet, and to do your own business, and to work with your hands —. (1 Thes. 4:11) We feel this is much needed advice now.

Study is from a word meaning be ambitious, used Rom. 15:20 (strived making it my aim) and 2 Cor. 5:9 (labour). This quietness is not a negative at ease in Zion attitude of unconcern. It is something set as a goal, something that requires positive planning and execution.

The Thessalonians had reacted to preaching about the second coming of Christ by ceasing daily ordinary activities, and engaging in hysterical, useless waiting — becoming a deadweight upon society and brethren. Our generation has their counterpart. The text says break it up. Quietness is a worthy ambition; work for it.

Lenski thinks to be quiet is, namely: to attend to your own business and to work with your hands even as, etc. It is the tranquility found in meaningful occupation; its counterpart being some that walk among you disorderly, that work not at all, but are busybodies. (2 Thes. 3:11) Luke uses the word four times: for rested (Lu. 23:56), and three times to indicate inward control, self-imposed peace. (Lu, 14:4; Acts 11:18; 21: 14) If we will grasp the self-imposed aspect of the word, we can see why Paul made it an ambition.

Christians need not expect a life free from trials (1 Pet. 4:12-f), nor void of struggle (1 Tim. 6:12). We pray for kings, etc., that we may lead a tranquil and quiet life, but this is not an indolent, self—indulgent life. We seek greater opportunity for service to God, conditions conductive to the spread of His word.

Our peace is that of the soldier who fights vigorously, with conviction that his cause is right and just. Our quietness is that of faith; the steadying influence, lest we beat the air. (1 Cor. 9:25-27)

Our problems will not be solved by youthful bluster or aged compromise. We Need Men Who Study To Be Quiet.

From PLAIN TALK, September 1970, pg. 1

CONTENTMENT

"For the love of money is a root of all sorts of evil and some by longing for it have wandered away from the faith and pierced themselves with many griefs."
— 1 Timothy 6:10

What do you want out of life? Family? Education? A career? A home of your own? All noble goals in and of themselves. But as Christians we would have to agree, they are secondary to our mission to please God. The blessing is, we can please God in any circumstance. As Paul illustrates in Philippians 4:11-13 from his own life, which was rarely comfortable, contentment comes from having a relationship with Jesus, not from altering our situation to find whatever our version of "happiness" might be at the moment.

Usually, in our society, "contentment" has to do with money. We always think we will be satisfied if we have a little bit more. Perhaps we think money is like junk food; as wonderful as each bite is, we convince ourselves we will know when we have had enough, and that we will stop then. But money doesn't have a saturation point. There is always more money to be earned, and more things on which to spend that money.

Paul says, "But godliness actually is a means of great gain when accompanied by contentment" (1 Timothy 6:6). It might seem to be contradictory to seek great gain by finding contentment. But of course, Paul isn't talking about any contentment that can be bought — or perhaps "rented" would be a better choice of words. He means spiritual gain. Here in the flesh, we have "every spiritual blessing in the heavenly places in Christ" (Ephesians 1:3). And eventually, in heaven, we will be blessed even more.

With that in mind, surely it is not too much for God to ask that we be satisfied with what we have, even if it is a bit less than what we would have wanted.

What are some ways the love of money can keep us from being content? _____

_____

_____

Further Reading

Erica says ...

I got accepted into medical school! I have always dreamed of being a doctor, and my parents have always encouraged me. But I have some concerns. I know some think it's not a good career for a Christian woman. And I know it puts a real strain on the other parts of your life, church included. And I want to have a family of my own one day. I guess I'm starting to have second thoughts.

What would you say to Erica?

_____

_____

_____

A Lesson from Your Bible—Luke 12:13-21

Have you ever been interrupted during something important to deal with something that was completely trivial? The Lord had one of those conversations one day. While explaining to His disciples the importance of standing up for their faith and confessing Him under threat of persecution, someone from the crowd decided to enlist His help in dividing up his father's inheritance. Apparently, he had not been left with enough possessions to suit him.

As usual, Jesus went straight to the heart of the matter. Greed is a far worse consideration than being shortchanged. Life is more than the things we put into it — especially since we won't be taking anything out of it.

To illustrate the point, He told a story about a farmer whose harvest had turned out to be too big. His initial impulse was not to praise God for His generosity or to find someone who was in need. No, he wanted to horde all of his goods so he would not have to work any longer. No more depending on God for the rain and the sunshine. All he would have to do is eat, drink, and be merry. Of course, he died that night, and all his plans went for nothing, along with his goods.

Too many blessings. How many of us could "complain" about the same thing? And how often is our "solution" the same as this farmer? More closet space. More square footage. More things to hold all of our things. The problem is not the things; it is our drive to acquire them and our need to possess them. Being consumed with materialism to the detriment of our soul makes us "the man who stores up treasure for himself, and is not rich toward God" (Luke 12:21).

God has promised to take care of us — not to the degree we would prefer, necessarily, but by giving us enough "food and covering." And if our true investment is in heaven anyway, what difference does it make if we must make do with a bit less here on earth? If, on the other hand, we constantly make financial decisions that have an obvious and negative effect on our service to Christ, is that not an indication that our priorities are out of alignment?

Jesus says, "For where your treasure is, there your heart will be also" (Luke 12:34). So where is your treasure?

How can we tell if we are greedy or selfish with our possessions?

_____

_____

_____

A Lesson from Your Elder

On my way out the door for college, my father told me, "Your expenses will expand to meet your income." He was right. Whatever money you may have will be spent in a day if you do not exercise control over it.

Pair your search for contentment with discipline. You may not be doing extremely well with either one at any given time. But perhaps a little discipline will buy you some time to find the rest of your contentment and vice versa.

I love you, and I'm praying for you.

> *O God and Father above,*
> *Give us this day our daily bread. And if You*
> *choose to give these young people more*
> *than that, please give them the wisdom*
> *they will need to use it to Your glory.*
> *In Jesus' name,*
> *Amen.*

From *PLAIN TALK*

Stuff About Things

"The love of money is a root of all kinds of evil" (1 Tim. 6:10), and the maker of all kinds of strange happenings. For example, in my early preaching days a group of elders told me they could support me only so much per week; "But," they added, "we have agreed you need not make any contributions from that amount." I asked if they had cleared this with the Lord — and saw some shamefaced men.

At another place I learned a man with oil wells had agreed to sign over royalty rights of a certain well to the church, so they could make double payments on their new building. But the church soon let up on their own giving, and were making single payments with the oil royalty money. The oil man wanted his well returned, but the elders refused to sign necessary papers.

In a regular business meeting, when it was asked, "Is there anything else?" I casually mentioned that I understood bro. ____ wanted to regain control of his well, and "whoever has those papers will want to fix that right away — for I'm sure none of us would try to force a man to give." There was a long silence, then one man said weakly, "Without that oil money we may lose our building." With all the seriousness I could muster I suggested we appoint a committee to look into school buildings, halls, or other places where we could meet when we were put out of our present house. Another long silence — then one of the elders said he knew where the papers were, and would see that they were signed and returned to the oil man. More shamefaced men!! But this story has a sequel. When the oil man got his well back, he took one look at the papers, thanked the brother, and again gave the well's earnings to the church, on a long-term basis.

Some will cheat the Lord in their computations of "as prospered." There are multiple cases of men stealing church money in the process of counting collections. Maybe that is why I remember so well the nine or ten year old boy who, hearing us talk of need for more money, called me aside to say he had $50 in savings, from the sale of some Future Farmer lambs; and he would give that for the Lord's work if I would get his father to check it out of the bank for him.

From PLAIN TALK, December 1982, pg. 8

UNASHAMED

"For this reason I also suffer these things, but I am not ashamed; for I know whom I have believed and I am convinced that He is able to guard what I have entrusted to Him until that day."

— 2 Timothy 1:12

If you have ever been arrested, it likely is a source of shame to you. Even if the charge was relatively trivial, even if you were innocent, it still makes you question the circumstances that led you to such an awkward and embarrassing situation. Some might have thought Paul was going through that sort of angst as he sat in prison for the second time (in Rome, that is — he had been imprisoned many other times in other places).

But Paul wanted Timothy to understand that he was not ashamed in the slightest of his behavior. The gospel was nothing of which he should be ashamed (Romans 1:16). In fact, three times in the first chapter of 2 Timothy Paul emphasizes how Christians should not be ashamed of their participation in the gospel, even if it costs them their freedom or (as was the case eventually for Paul) their lives.

Paul was willing to suffer the loss of all things (Philippians 3:7-8) because the things he truly valued (his spiritual treasures) were being guarded by Jesus (Matthew 6:20). He had lived most of his life not knowing Jesus. But in his final months of life, he knew Him enough to put full confidence in Him. This was despite the fact that trusting in Jesus had landed him in prison (again) and was about to cost him his life literally.

As we should not be ashamed of ourselves, we also ought not to be ashamed of those who suffer as Paul did. The "support" of Phygelus and Hermogenes appears to have dwindled with Paul's fortunes. Onesiphorus' family, though, made a special effort to seek Paul out to render aid when he needed it most. Truly, our state of heart shows in what we do for those who can do nothing for us in return — and reflects the true state of our heart regarding the Lord Himself (Matthew 25:34-40).

Further Reading

Matthew
11:10-32, 39

Luke 9:21-26

What are some situations in which we may feel ashamed of the gospel?

_____

_____

Doug says ...

Most of my denominational "Christian" friends make their position on Jesus pretty obvious. They put decals and bumper stickers on their cars, they wear Jesus-themed T-shirts, one of them even got John 3:16 tattooed on his back—the whole verse. I don't want to be doing my deeds to be seen of men. Still, I can't help thinking that they are more vocal in their mistaken beliefs than I am in my beliefs. Should I be more obvious with my religion?

What would you say to Doug?

_____

_____

_____

A Lesson from Your Bible—Daniel 6

Most of us know the story of how Daniel refused to discontinue his habit of praying toward Jerusalem three times daily in his open window. We know how the advisers of Darius, who ruled over the Medes and Persians in Babylon, counseled the king to make it a capital offense to pray to any man or god for 30 days. We know how they did it specifically to trap Daniel, and that it worked. And, of course, we know how Daniel was thrown into the lions' den as a result, and how God delivered him.

What we don't know, and what we may have found ourselves asking from time to time, is this: Would it have been wrong for Daniel to take a month off from his routine? Or could he have continued his prayers, just with his window closed? After all, the Law of Moses is silent regarding how often prayers should be offered or what form they should take.

But whether Daniel could have gotten away with less is not the point. He knew the law had been passed specifically because of his public prayer habits. He knew that his detractors believed he would go so far as even to defy the king if asked to compromise. That was precisely what made it impossible for him not to compromise. To change his habits would be a message: Daniel will back down from his convictions if he is in fear for his life. That was a message Daniel was, literally, willing to die to avoid sending. Much like the case with Daniel's friends Shadrach, Meshech, and Abednego in Daniel 3:16-18, Daniel does not appear to have had any advanced word about God's protection. He simply continued serving God as he had, because it was the right thing to do; and he submitted to the judgment of the king because it was the right thing to do. His deliverance from the mouths of lions is a reminder to us even today that our service to God is nothing of which we should be ashamed. We are Christians, and we are proud to let our neighbors know about it.

At what point, if ever, can public service to God do as much or more harm than good? Cite Scripture.

_____

_____

_____

A Lesson from Your Elder

You probably have already run into people who have tried to belittle your faith. It may have been a friend. It may have been a mentor, such as a teacher or professor. Being a Christian is not always the popular position to take.

It is, however, the right position. Embarrassment may come to you, perhaps from not participating in the sin of the moment, or defending the Bible against attack, or going the extra mile (even literally) to be with the people of God on the Lord's Day. But whatever discomfort may be yours to bear in the short term is just that much more spiritual treasure you are storing away for yourself in heaven.

I love you, and I'm praying for you.

> *O God and Father above,*
> *We know the pressure to give in to sin,*
> *and spiritual compromise is great. Please*
> *give our young people a greater portion*
> *of faith, so that they will be able to with-*
> *stand in the day of trial. Help them devote*
> *themselves to study of Your word, where*
> *that faith can be found. Help them be*
> *proud of the Name they wear*
> *In Jesus' name,*
> *Amen.*

From PLAIN TALK

Poor Misteated You!!

Paul wrote fourteen of the twenty-seven books of the New Testament. It is a marvelous tribute to his character that one may read these books and not think of Paul as a sour, disgruntled, self-pitying man; for his life as a Christian was one long string of persecutions and heart-aches.

He was baptized in Damascus; and shortly thereafter, had to be let down the wall in a basket to escape would-be murderers. (2 Cor. 11:32) Coming to Jerusalem; disciples feared and refused him. Finally accepted, he preached -- until he had to flee for his life. (Acts 9:22-30) From Tarsus, he came to Antioch -- to become soon embroiled in dissension and disputation with false brethren. (Acts 15:1)

Journeying to foreign lands to preach the gospel, he was stoned and dragged from the city as dead; (Acts 14:19) and this was but one incident in a lifetime of persecutions, beatings, imprisonment's, scorn and trial. (2 Cor. 1:8-9 6:4-5) "But we had the sentence of death in ourselves, that we should not trust in ourselves, but in God which raiseth the dead."

I know brethren today who, being falsely accused of something, or have their work, word or motive questioned; want to fight back carnally or else withdraw into their corner to nurse their supposed great wounds. Paul would never have "gotten to first base" had he followed such a course. He wrote, "All that will live godly in Christ Jesus shall suffer persecution." (2 Tim. 3:10-12) When a man decides to preach the pure gospel of Christ, he decides to endure hardship.

Seems to me he ought to know that, if he knows much about the work of the preacher as outlined in the Bible. It seems equally clear that any Christian who goes into the Christian life with eyes wide open, counts a like cost, and accepts it openly. ("all that will live godly." See Lu.14:26) I CAN'T SEE THAT ANY OF US HAVE ANY LEGITIMATE "KICK A-COMING."

Many assign Paul's troubles to the pagans, and the "wicked world" of his times. But Paul names "perils among false brethren" and "the care of all the churches" among his burdens. It is significant to me that he "brought trouble upon himself" because of his great, unselfish concern for the spiritual welfare of others. (2 Cor.11:23 -f. 7:5-6) Yet he had to say, "The more abundantly I love you, the less I be loved." (2 Cor. 12:15) This too is a role all workers for Christ must willingly accept.

Brethren falsely accused him, said he was "crazy." (2 Cor.5:12-13 11:16) "His letters, say they, are weighty and powerful; but his bodily presence is weak, and his speech contemptible." (2 Cor. 10:10) Brother, can you take it?? Sister, will you endure??

I can name you dozens of brethren who have compromised their convictions, quit preaching, ceased to oppose known errors, or quit the Lord altogether, because of some slight persecution. Someone laughed at them, or made a slighting remark, or failed to pay them proper respect. "If any man suffers as a Christian, let him not be ashamed; but let him glorify God on this behalf." (1 Pet. 4:16)

From PLAIN TALK, July 1967, pg. 5

HARDSHIP

"Suffer hardship with me, as a good soldier of Christ Jesus."

— 2 Timothy 2:3

Nothing worthwhile in life comes easy. We hear that a lot, particularly from older ones who are trying to encourage us to persevere through hardship. But is it true? Certainly, it may seem from the outside looking in that certain ones have a much easier time getting what they want — perhaps because of their upbringing or family wealth, perhaps because of an abundance of natural talent, perhaps because of sheer luck.

Success in Jesus Christ, though, is different. Paul likens it to being in an army. Surely anyone who enlists in the military anticipates a rough road. Admittedly, some will encounter more life-threatening situations than others. But the lifestyle of a soldier implies a certain degree of hardship. But the volunteer soldier goes even so, as he sees the benefits to service as outweighing the freedom he is surrendering. Once enlisted, he makes a special effort to keep from being caught up in "the affairs of everyday life" (2 Timothy 2:4). The more focus he places on life's niceties, the more dissatisfied with his service he becomes. So he protects himself from discouragement by focusing on the task at hand.

Beyond that, the Christian should be focusing on the reward that awaits. An athlete anticipates the prize for his success; a farmer hopes for a good harvest. So also the Christian can endure life's difficulties because Jesus has promised eternal glory for the faithful.

Paul is perhaps quoting a First Century hymn in 2 Timothy 2:11-13. The words remind us not to be satisfied with simply joining forces with Jesus; we must endure if we are to reign. The assurance that Jesus will be faithful in His commitment to us should encourage us to be equally faithful in our commitment to Him.

Further Reading

Psalm 40

Revelation 2:1-11

1 Peter 4:12-19

What are some hardships with which we have to deal? What are some things we can do to help us endure? _____

_____

_____

Erica says ...

I've been reading the Psalms a lot lately. There's lots of talk about God lifting the believer up, defeating his enemies, blessing him with life and success. I do not see much of that these days. I asked the preacher, and he said most of the blessings we get from God are of a spiritual nature. But that's not the message I'm getting from what I read in the Bible. Is God with me or not?

What would you say to Erica?

_____

_____

_____

A Lesson from Your Bible—1 Kings 19

Elijah's lowest low immediately followed his highest high. We read in 1 Kings 18 how he challenged King Ahab and his prophets on Mount Carmel. Fire consumed Elijah's sacrifice, not Baal's. The people, whom Elijah had accused of wavering between the two gods, shouted, "The LORD, He is God; the LORD, He is God" (1 Kings 18:39). To cap things off, the people put the false prophets to death, and rain came back to the land after three years of severe drought.

One would think this would have had a transforming effect on Ahab and his wife, Jezebel. Instead, they were all the more emboldened to take Elijah's life. While the sounds of celebration were still in the air, Elijah was running for his life.

Forty days later, he found himself at Horeb, the mountain of God. God found him there and asked, "What are you doing here, Elijah?" Elijah proceeded to tell God all his problems — how he had been so zealous for the cause, how he had gotten no support, how he was now left alone. So God told him to "stand on the mountain before the LORD" (1 Kings 19:11). Elijah went, no doubt expecting some tremendous demonstration of God's presence. But His presence was not in the strong wind, or the earthquake, or the fire. He only left his post after hearing "a sound of a gentle blowing," which appeared to connote the presence of God more than the spectacles he had seen before.

We tend to think our hardships should be answered with demonstrations from God that are as visible as the hardships themselves; and sometimes, as was the case at Mount Carmel, they are. But often we are asked to see the presence of God in the small things in life. God had given Elijah food for the journey and allowed him to subsist on it for 40 days. He gave Elijah a mission — to anoint his successor as well as the next kings of Israel and Aram. And he also gave him some perspective. He was not as alone as he imagined himself to be; there were still 7,000 who had not bowed to Baal.

Hardship comes with the job. With God's help, we will not get so distracted by how we think the job is going that we cease to do it.

What should we pray in times of trouble?

_____

_____

_____

A Lesson from Your Elder

It's easy to assume that, since you love and serve the God of all creation, He will be there for you to make your load lighter in troubled times. He has done so for countless others, after all. But He won't do it for you every time; in fact, in your darkest hours, you may wonder if He has ever helped you at all.

Do not doubt the Father's love for you. Remember the investment of love He has already made in you at the cross. Remember the glories above that far outweigh the difficulties of life below. You can do this. Be patient, and be strong.

I love you, and I'm praying for you.

> *O God and Father above,*
> *Give us this day our daily bread. And if You*
> *choose to give these young people more*
> *than that, please give them the wisdom*
> *they will need to use it to Your glory.*
> *In Jesus' name,*
> *Amen.*

From PLAIN TALK

The Moment of Truth

From the Spanish bull-ring, where the cool nerve, the Matador has long been regarded with national pride, comes the expression, "moment of truth."

El Toro and the man! The massive beast, nostrils aflare, goaded to hot fury, perhaps symbolic of all man's foe, is ready to drive a cruel horn into his vitals. In previous charges, the man has led the bull closer and closer with the cape -- but always to pass. Now the beast must be brought to ground. Skillfully the sword must be placed so that the maddened rush of the bull drives the blade to its destiny. With this savage lunge, the beast dies or sweeps el Matador aside in a crushing mingle of blood and dust.

The flashing caps, the splendid uniform, the wild cheers of the packed stadium --- all glorious, but none kill the bull. Boasts of billboards, expecta-tions of the sports writers -- all meaningless now. It is the awful "moment of truth." The man is truly El Matador --- "the killer" --- or is swept to igno-minious defeat. As I contemplate this spectacle, I realize how surely we all face our "moment of truth." This generation has scarcely known hardship. Depression is meaningful only to grandparents; and the horrors of war are seen as foreign products, by citizens of a powerful winning nation. How would we face a disastrous national crisis?

We have posed as Christians. Baptized into Christ, we "attend" church, sing, pray, and partake. We say we love God, and acknowledge that God must come first; but rarely is our dedication to this principle fully tested. What knowledge, what moral fiber have we developed by which to meet our spiritual "moment of truth?"

When our practice is questioned, do we become angry? Is our defense the flimsy garment of tradition? El Toro cuts swiftly through such. Are we artful winners of our own "straw" arguments? One day we must face a genuine foe. Do we judge ourselves by ourselves? One day God will judge us in righteousness, for eternity; and we will face an awesome, irrevocable and final "moment of truth."

From PLAIN TALK, November 1964, pg. 1

HANDLING THE WORD

"Be diligent to present yourself approved to God as a workmen who does not need to be ashamed, accurately handling the word of truth."

— 2 Timothy 2:15

The English language has left the King James Version of the Bible behind in many areas. A good example is 2 Timothy 2:15. The word "study" in the KJV does not mean to read, or even to read carefully. It has to do more with a Christian's devotion to his calling. "Be diligent," reads the New American Standard Bible, and other versions read similarly. Likewise the archaic "rightly dividing" is rendered "accurately handling." Some Bible class teachers use 2 Timothy 2:15 to teach young children how to "rightly divide" the New Testament from the Old Testament. That is one way to properly "handle" God's word, certainly, but is not the main point.

Paul is telling Timothy that his calling, both as a Christian and as an evangelist, requires him to apply himself intently to the task. It is work, absolutely. And the best way to do it — the only way, really — is to know the Bible thoroughly and to be skilled in its usage.

God's word shows God what kind of person we are when He splits us open with it (Hebrews 4:12-13). Likewise, it shows anyone who cares to pay attention. Some will ignore God's word. Others will abuse it for their purposes (2 Peter 3:16). But the workman of whom God approves must be seen, both by Him and by the workman's neighbors, as one who is comfortable enough with the word to use it frequently, fairly, honestly, and in a timely fashion.

It was said of Eleazar, one of David's mighty men, that he fought so hard that "his hand was weary and clung to the sword" (2 Samuel 23:8-10). Would that it could be said of us that we fought so effectively with "the sword of the Spirit, which is the word of God" (Ephesians 6:17) that it clung to our hands.

Further Reading

Psalm 119

Ephesians 6:10-17

How might we handle God's word other than "accurately?" Give examples.

_____

_____

Doug says ...

I get called names a lot. One of my denomina-tional friends calls me a Campbellite; I don't even know what that means, although he seems to think I do. A friend who attends another church of Christ in town said I'm an "anti." I'm quite sure he doesn't know what that means. Maybe I'm not too sure myself. Anyway, it seems like a pretty lazy way to discuss the Bible.

What would you say to Doug?

_____

_____

_____

A Lesson from Your Bible—Matthew 4:1-11

Knowing the Bible is important. Using it, even more so. But as the devil proved in his encounter with the Lord in the wilderness, that may not be enough.

The first of the three temptations offered Jesus was pertaining to the lust of the flesh. After fasting for 40 days, He was hungry. Satan suggested He make stones into bread. Jesus, though, wanted to emphasize His depen-dence on His Father for sustenance rather than going it alone. In keeping with that, He quoted Scripture — Deuteronomy 8:3, to be precise.

As if to say, "Two can play that game," the devil cited Scripture himself in the second temptation. He brought Jesus to the pinnacle of the temple and challenged Him to throw Himself down. He cited Psalm 91:11 in so doing, suggesting that the approved one of God in the psalm would be protected from all harm by God's angels. But Jesus said the challenge itself was an affront to God. "You shall not put the LORD your God to the test," He said, citing Deuteronomy 6:16. His point was not that "His Scripture" somehow canceled out "Satan's Scripture," but rather that the one put the other in a proper context. God's promise of protection was not given to us so that we could intentionally put ourselves in harm's way but rather to give us hope and confidence in a world fraught with difficulty.

Psalm 91 is poetry, as is the rest of the Psalms and many other parts of the Bible. That is not to say it is to be discounted at all, but rather to acknowledge that its style of communication is very different from, say, the legal code of Leviticus or the historical narrative of Joshua. Truth given in figurative language is still truthful, but that does not mean every sentence should be accepted as a literal direction for our lives; otherwise, Psalm 91 would have us playing with vipers and lions.

The requirements God has for His people are typically given in straightforward language. It should be considered axiomatic that we should never abandon the clear teaching of the text because of a notion we derived from a figurative passage. Any reasonable reader would have known Satan's use of Psalm 91 was misguided, and that Jesus' reference to Deuteronomy 6 was on point.

What are some other passages of Scripture that you have heard taken out of context? Explain how they should be properly used.

_____

_____

_____

A Lesson from Your Elder

Read your Bible. Surely I'm not the first person to tell you that. Read it daily. Read it dutifully. Read it with a view to application.

But don't think that you are any closer to God or His will for your life simply because you have a Bible open in front of you. Plenty of people read the Bible daily and ignore what it tells them. Get in the habit of reading and re-reading. Challenge yourself. Ask questions of people more experienced than you.

I love you, and I'm praying for you.

O God and Father above,
We praise you for the gift of Your word,
preserved for us through the ages and
made available for us today. Bless us as
we read. Give us wisdom to know its truth,
courage in its application, and persistence
as we face the opposition.
In Jesus' name,
Amen.

From *PLAIN TALK*

Necessary Inference

We do not know who first used the expression "necessary inference" but its equivalent is found in works of Aristotle and other Greek teachers of the reasoning process. When evidence is collected and we draw a conclusion, the conclusion is our inference. It is necessary to the extent the evidence demands it. There is a colloquial use of inference, i.e., surmise, guess, hint, etc. but this is not its use in legitimate discussion of reasoning and Bible authority.

I would charitably assume that any gospel preacher knows that God made His will known to man by sending His Holy Spirit to chosen messengers, to guide them in speaking and writing what He wanted us to know. It seems uncharitable to have to say that this inspired message is understandable, for God's process of imparting information is thwarted if it is not. But how does man understand the Bible? Exactly as he understands any other written message. He must be able to read — to translate words into mental images. He accumulates information, contemplates, reasons, and draws conclusions. These conclusions are inferred in the strict and logical meaning of the term.

The inspired history written by Luke records that Peter commanded some people in Jerusalem to repent and be baptized. This is related to God's promise to those afar off. We have sufficient evidence to conclude that this was a portion of the message Christ wanted proclaimed to every creature so we necessarily infer that we also must repent and be baptized. Our understanding is the result of a process of human reasoning upon the word God.

That reasoning can be true and productive of good (2 Tim. 2:15; Eph. 3:4) or it can be faulty and productive of bad (2 Pet. 3:16); depending upon the attitude and purpose one has in approaching God's word (Jn. 7:17). We may infer without sufficient evidence — and that is why evidence is prefixed to inference when discussing Bible interpretation. We are individually responsible before our use of His message.

But the miracle of revelation in the giving and confirming, not in the process of reception. God made the man, for whom He made the word.

Is a necessary inference binding upon the conscience? Yes! When careful study of God's word impresses with an inescapable conclusion, ever conveyed, you must receive it or be untrue to yourself and to God.

From PLAIN TALK, August 1975, pg. 2

CLEANSING

"Therefore, if anyone cleanses himself from these things, he will be a vessel for honor, sanctified, useful to the Master, prepared for every good work."
— 2 Timothy 2:21

Thanksgiving dinner is rarely served in Tupperware containers. That is not to speak ill of Tupperware but rather to emphasize the difference between various vessels in a typical kitchen. Better vessels are used for special occasions. Poor ones may be used to store nails, collect kitchen grease, or even feed pets.

Paul uses this metaphor to show why a gospel preacher such as Timothy should not devote himself to lesser causes. "These things" of which Timothy was to cleanse himself (2 Timothy 2:21) seems to refer to the "worldly and empty chatter" noted a few verses earlier — the "foolish and ignorant speculations" of verse 23. Timothy was not to get bogged down in "religious" debates that have little or nothing to do with the gospel, and that threaten to fracture the body of Christ. If all Timothy had to work within a particular location were lesser materials (1 Corinthians 3:12-14), that would not be held to Timothy's account.

Youthful lusts can lead us down the wrong road. As discussed earlier, a quest for prominence or reputation might lead a young person to chase doctrinal rabbits. But to "call on the Lord from a pure heart" is a simple matter. It just requires enough faith in God to trust in His word, enough love for others to share it with kindness, and enough patience and gentleness to persist in doing so.

Paul had not yet given up on all the wooden and earthenware vessels in the church. They could still "come to their senses and escape the snare of the devil" if they could do as Timothy was to do: wash ourselves of any tendencies toward egotism, and "pursue righteousness, faith, love, and peace."

Further Reading

1 Corinthians
3:10-15

Ephesians 5:1-13

Philippians 4:8

What does it mean to "call on the Lord" or to "name the name of the Lord?" Can it be done wrongly? Explain. _____

_____

_____

_____

Erica says ...

If I were to be completely honest, I would have to say my efforts at fleeing "youthful lusts" are erratic at best. I'm lazy. I complain too much. I make excuses for myself. I don't think about spiritual things enough. I want to get better, but sometimes it seems like I will never be the kind of Christian that I want to be. Oh, that's another thing. I'm impatient.

What would you say to Erica?

_____

_____

_____

A Lesson from Your Bible—Nehemiah 13

"Remember me, O my God, for good." This is the oft-repeated refrain from Nehemiah's memoir of his work in Jerusalem. Against a great deal of opposition, he led the nation in the reconstruction of the city of Jerusalem, especially the walls. While so doing, he helped his countrymen build back their sense of national identity. This meant far more than just defense against physical enemies; Nehemiah was just as concerned, if not more so, with the moral decay from within that threatened to erode away their character.

Nehemiah returned to his old position with the Persian emperor in Susa for a period of time. He left instructions regarding the land, and then returned years later to check on the nation's progress. Unfortunately, the people had regressed in all three of the areas Nehemiah had designated.

Firstly, the function of the temple had been desecrated. Foreign influences had been permitted within restricted areas, and functionaries such as the Levites and singers had not been compensated, forcing them to abandon their tasks. Quickly Nehemiah reprimanded those who were responsible and put the things in order.

Secondly, the sabbath was being desecrated. From the beginning of the nation, no work had been permitted on the seventh day of the week (Exodus 20:8-11). But in a rush to reestablish the nation's economic base, traders and merchants had brought their wares to Jerusalem daily, including the sabbath. Nehemiah barred the gates of the city to all commerce as soon as the sabbath began. Some merchants spent the night outside the gate, perhaps thinking Nehemiah would relent. He did not permit this either, even threatening them with force.

Thirdly, he condemned those who had intermarried with foreigners. Historically this had led to idolatry among the people — the very sin for which Babylon punished them for 70 years. Nehemiah reminded them of Solomon's foreign wives and the trouble they made for him. He lamented the fact that many of Judah's children could not speak their language, speaking the language of Ashdod instead. If this was to be the nation of God, it would have to cleanse itself of all the speech, habits and associations that would call their commitment to God into question.

What associations should we "cleanse" ourselves of as Christians?

_____

_____

A Lesson from Your Elder

Have you ever washed your hands after a particularly grimy job, only to realize they weren't entirely clean yet? It may take a few tries. It may take some scrubbing with a rag or nail brush. But if your mother is like mine, you won't come to the dinner table until the job is complete.

Cleansing our lives is even harder. After some failed efforts, we may decide "a little dirt never hurt anyone." That's dirty thinking from a dirty mind. You can do better.

I love you, and I'm praying for you.

> *O God and Father above,*
> *Give our young people a love of Your*
> *truth, and a contempt for all that poses as*
> *Your truth. Encourage them in their pursuit*
> *of it, and help them receive Your discipline*
> *in a meek and humble manner.*
> *In Jesus' name,*
> *Amen.*

From *PLAIN TALK*

Stuff About Things

The gristly old Texas Ranger sat patiently, tolerantly; chewing his tobacco and waiting while the doctor bound a gunshot wound.

"Three against one!" someone said, "and yet you walked right into their guns and took them all. How could you do such a thing?"

The reply was one part philosophy and many parts faith. "*Ain't nobody in the wrong can stand again a man in the right, that keeps on a-comin'!*"

PLAIN TALK hasn't "gone western" -- we just like the slant of this thing. The first step is to be "right." Many fears and frustrations are but proofs that we lack conviction -- perhaps suspect that we are wrong. Not all who ignore our invitation to discuss Bible differences are cowards; some are without ammunition.

Bro. Foy E. Wallace, Jr. used to say certain brethren did not debate for the same reason a muley refuses to "hook horns." (For the sake of our city folk, that reason is "no horns.") People who are "right" -- or have conscientious convictions that they have Bible authority for their practices -- are usually happy to discuss issues.

Being right in religion means to conform to the truth of God -- to have divine authority for our faith and practice. It presupposes an attitude all too rare, even among brethren; a desire to "prove all things; hold fast that which is good." This attitude welcomes investigation and assures a fair, objective consideration of all pertinent information.

In brief, it puts into practice, among brethren, the thing we frequently criticize the denominations for not doing. Physician, heal thyself!!

"That keeps on a-comin'!" After all, God is a majority. If God be for us, who can be against us? (Rom. 8:31) The confidence of the faithful is not dependent upon numbers, fine buildings, or other status symbols. opposition is taken in stride - and they "keep on a-comin'" because they place their trust in God, not in man. "The foundation of God standeth sure, having this seal: The Lord knoweth them that are His. And, Let every one that nameth the name of Christ depart from iniquity." (2 Tim. 2:19)

Those faithful to God will triumph; often in this life, always in eternity. All others must "go that-a-way!"

From PLAIN TALK, July 1966, pg. 8

LEARNING

"For among them are those who enter into households and captivate weak women weighed down with sins, led on by various impulses, always learning and never able to come to the knowledge of the truth."

— 2 Timothy 3:6-7

Education is good. If you went to college, or are in college now someone — either you, your parents, or the taxpayers — paid a great deal of money to get you educated in one discipline or another. As they used to say on the commercials, "A mind is a terrible thing to waste."

Education is just like any other earthly objective to be attained. Education, money, prestige, friendships, entertainment — these all have their place in life here on earth, and none is inherently good or evil; however, their real importance is in whether they are used to pull us toward God or push us further from God.

Education is particularly problematical in that it builds self-confidence and self-sufficiency — traits that can easily lead to pride. If we get used to puzzling our way through life's difficulties, we can imagine ourselves capable of constructing our spiritual solutions apart from God and His word. We can even convince ourselves we need no saving at all. Such is a recipe for spiritual disaster.

It is generally thought that Jannes and Jambres were the prophets of Egypt who opposed Moses before Pharaoh. They were able somehow to partially duplicate the feat of turning a wooden staff into a serpent. But even in their "success," they failed; their serpents were swallowed by Aaron's. It could be that the prophets had devised a way of immobilizing a snake temporarily; some believe Satan may have been able to grant them some limited supernatural power. But as always, the main effect of Satan's power, other than to beguile the gullible, is to show God's superiority.

God's ways will always overcome.

Further Reading

1 Corinthians
1:18-31

Ecclesiastes
1:12-18;
12:9-14

In what specific ways can learning interfere with our walk with Christ? ____

_____

_____

_____

Doug says ...

I am a third-year geology student. Naturally, evolution vs. creationism comes up occasionally. I tried to make my point about science supporting the Biblical record in my last visit to the professor's office. I think he's finally lost patience with me, though. He said, nicely but firmly, no one was going to get a degree in his department if he calls himself a creationist. And he's the department head.

What would you say to Doug?

_____

_____

_____

A Lesson from Your Bible—Job 42:1-17

More than anything, Job wanted answers. He wanted to understand. And most of us would have been the same way. Going through what he was going through, having his family and friends turn on him, having his commitment to God challenged, none of it made any sense. He knew his faith. He knew he had not denied God. And his understanding of the workings of God did not mesh with his circumstances.

But Job did not need more information. He needed to appreciate properly the information he already had. He knew about God's sovereignty, God's power, God's connection with His creation, God's justice. He knew he would stand justified before Him when the time came (Job 19:25-27). But he still wanted an opportunity to argue before God (Job 13:15). He thought that perhaps things would make more sense if God were to explain things to him more completely if He could be persuaded to fill in the gaps of Job's knowledge.

The irony is, Job was very much correct in believing there was more going on than met the eye. Job was being specifically tested by Satan to see if he would hold to his faith in difficult circumstances (Job 1-2). If God had given him that information in the midst of his woes, Job might have found some solace.

But that's not the way it works sometimes. Sometimes the lesson is not that we need to figure out why God is doing what He is doing, but rather to have faith that His ways are best and that we are safe in His hands. For the better part of 42 chapters, Job does nothing but ask for God to educate him in His ways, and God refuses to do that. He tells him to have faith, and He rebukes him when that faith wavers.

It is tempting to look to secular education to explain the actions of God — how He parted the Red Sea, whether manna is a naturally occurring phenomenon, etc. But if we were to conclusively prove, as some have suggested, that the ten plagues of Egypt were the result of a volcanic eruption in southern Europe, that would not make the Bible any more authoritative. And we might start thinking other miracles, such as Jesus' resurrection, can be "explained away" as well.

Can God use natural forces to give mankind signs? If so, does that make the signs less significant or God less powerful? Explain.

_____

_____

A Lesson from Your Elder

I have a college education, and I hope my daughters get theirs as well. A degree provides opportunities in this life, as well as life experiences that have value in and of themselves. But I equipped them with the truth they really need through God's word. We have taken great pains along the way to emphasize the priority of Biblical knowledge. No thoughts of man can invalidate the thoughts of God.

So get educated. But don't get too smart for your good. God won't check your curriculum vitae at the pearly gates, I assure you.

I love you, and I'm praying for you.

> O God and Father above,
> We praise you for who You are, and also
> for who we are — Your special creation,
> made in Your image, capable of bettering
> ourselves and of choosing the best way to
> do so. Help us choose Your way so we can
> truly be Your children.
> In Jesus' name,
> Amen.

From PLAIN TALK

Stuff About Things

A friend of mine, discussing a sermon she had heard and enjoyed, said she was surprised that this particular preacher did so well, because "he had a good education."

That's no misprint. She was surprised that sermon of value could come from one highly educated. Nor is my friend a victim of ignorant superstition. She values secular education. But experience had taught her that "degrees" have a way of pushing into the foreground, so that sermons become pedantic and real spiritual concern for lost souls is overshadowed. Plain, old-fashioned Bible preaching is not good enough for Dr. Rev.; and what suits him doesn't stir the heart of the man who needs salvation.

Several years ago on a Sunday when a sore throat would not permit me to speak, two college boys were invited to "fill in." I heard both sermons, and later the two boys came to my office and asked for my criticisms.

One boy (we'll call him Joe) had the makings of an after-dinner speaker. He had personality - plus, a few jokes, illustrations from current events and sports, and just enough emotional appeal to make his "talk" sound like preaching. I knew he had "gone over great" with the crowd. The other (call him Dan) showed "stage fright" and spoke in a halting, half-stutter. But he had compiled a fine list of scriptures on his subject, and used his time reading and explaining them, and making direct application to the hearers. I tried to make a fair and encouraging report to the boys; but told Joe that he was on the wrong track. I urged him to use his talents to present the Word, not himself; to warn people of their sin and damnation, and make them know his concern. Joe thought this was "out of date."

Both boys graduated from an outstanding "Christian" college, married, and chose secular jobs. But Joe has now joined a denomination, where fun, frolic, and "youth devotionals" are substituted for Christianity. Dan is teaching a Bible class in a sound church, preaches as he has opportunity, and grows stronger day by day.

Fault of the college? Not per se. But one boy succumbed to the modern "social gospel" concept of Christianity, and one had faith in God's word.

From PLAIN TALK, April 1965, pg. 8

PERSECUTION

"Indeed, all who desire to live godly in Christ Jesus will be persecuted."
— 2 Timothy 3:12

It would be nice to tell you persecution was a First Century phenomenon, that the underpinnings of American society assure us that we will be safe in our free exercise of religion for the indefinite future and that episodes of discomfort in the Lord's service today are situational, minor and infrequent. But I can't tell you that.

I can tell you that God's commands are manageable (1 John 5:3) and that opportunities to obey will be provided (1 Corinthians 10:13), and that you have your brethren at the ready to assist you when times are difficult (Galatians 6:2). But persecution is real, even here in America. And it could very conceivably get much worse in the near future.

Forces are at work now, both within and without the government, to eat away at the very heart of our practice of faith. Other practitioners see Christians as the enemy, to be converted at the tip of the sword. Atheists see Jesus as a primary source of the world's problems; they think that emphasizing eternity over this life keeps us from fixing earthly problems and that accepting universal "truth" as revealed in the Bible interferes with the pursuit of earthly pleasures. They are determined to bring the church down but have lacked opportunity in the past. That may not be the case for long.

We cannot trust in government or a "religious" society to lessen the burdens of life as a Christian. Instead, we must grow our faith so that we can withstand any onslaught of persecution that may arise.

And incidentally, we often do a poor job of simply bearing up under the strain we face today. If we cower before unarmed friends and coworkers when our faith is challenged, can we expect to do better when guns are in our faces?

Further Reading

Luke 22:54-62

Revelation 2:8-11

What persecutions do Christians in other parts of the world face today? Is their situation harder than ours? Explain. _____

_____

_____

_____

Erica says ...

I don't know if "persecution" is a fair word to describe what I go through as a Christian. I get left out of things sometimes. Occasionally I am mocked in a lighthearted way because I don't drink or curse. But it's easily manageable. My life isn't disrupted much. A lot of Christians have it much worse than I do. Am I doing something wrong? Am I supposed to be suffering more than this?

What would you say to Erica?

_____

_____

_____

A Lesson from Your Bible—Jeremiah 20

Jeremiah earned his nickname, "The weeping prophet." He spent years preaching to a nation that was actively opposed to his message, finding few supporters and many detractors — including the royal family and most of the priesthood. At one point a priest named Pashhur had Jeremiah beaten and put in stocks overnight for daring to suggest God would bring judgment against Jerusalem. Of course, this was not Jeremiah's wish; this was God's message. But Pashhur and most of his countrymen were not interested in hearing that; they wanted to hear, "Peace, peace," instead of walking in the "ancient paths" (Jeremiah 6:14-17).

This episode was almost too much for Jeremiah. The people's absolute refusal to listen — indeed, their mockery at his attempts to save them — almost drove him to abandon his post. Ultimately, though, he was committed to God and God's mission for his life; he would not waver from it, regardless of circumstances. As he wrote in Jeremiah 20:9, "But if I say, 'I will not remember Him or speak anymore in His name,' then in my heart it becomes like a burning fire shut up in my bones; and I am weary of holding it in, and I cannot endure it."

Jeremiah's situation would not improve as the months and years pro-gressed; very much the opposite, in fact. Surely he continued to have days when he wondered why he had even been born, what purpose his life was serving. But through it all, he continued to see his God as his "dread champion" (Jeremiah 20:11), an unseen ally in his battle with the doubters and detractors. It must have seemed on a day-to-day basis that he was not accomplishing anything, that his suffering was meaningless. But the book of Jeremiah mentions men such as Ebed-melech and Baruch who supported him and, no doubt, benefited from his good example. And his cause was ultimately vindicated. Today we can read his book and reap the benefits of his experience and wisdom. Although God will not inspire us to write a book of His words as He did Jeremiah, we too can leave behind a legacy of faith and determination that will inspire others.

What can we do to keep our spirits up while we wait for our persecution to lessen?

_____

_____

A Lesson from Your Elder

You don't know yet how good you have it. I know, because I don't know yet either, and I have a few decades' head start. Maybe one day we will have to go through the same trials our brethren of old endured, and then we will look back on "the good old days" with fondness.

In the meantime, though, take advantage of the opportunities you have. Speak boldly when there are few and minor consequences. It would be tough to learn how to speak boldly in tough times if we learned to give ourselves plenty of excuses in easy times.

I love you, and I'm praying for you.

> *O God and Father above,*
> *We don't know what the future holds. But*
> *we know You hold the future. We place*
> *ourselves in Your hands to do with as You*
> *see fit. Whether these young people have*
> *good times or bad ahead, help them to*
> *trust in You through it all. Help them focus*
> *on our heavenly home, and be bold to*
> *walk the course You have marked for us to*
> *go.*
> *In Jesus' name,*
> *Amen.*

From PLAIN TALK

Stuff About Things

We are finally convinced that personal work, one-on-one, is the best way to teach our neighbor the gospel, so we call on our friendly barber who lives just down the street. He greets us with a smile, and the conversation goes something like this.

"Glad to see you, Reverend! I have intended to talk with you for some time but...." But, we cut him off—.

"If you read your Bible you would know that 'Holy and Reverend is God's name' (Psm. 111:9), and we should not give flattering titles to any man."

"Sorry, Pastor. I just meant..." "Pastor? Don't you know 'pastor' means 'shepherd,' and the shepherds of a church are the bishops? I'm no pastor, I'm just a soul-loving preacher, taking the blessed gospel to poor lost souls in this wicked world."

"Well now, uh... preacher, I didn't mean any harm. You see in our church we... "

"OUR church? You folk talk about YOUR church as if the Lord didn't have a church. The church belongs to Jesus Christ, who purchased it with His precious blood. The churches men have planted will all be rooted up."

If he runs us out of the house, we can always report our "persecution" at the Personal Work Meeting, and counter adverse criticism by saying, "We really told him the truth."

Civil courtesy would solve many of these problems. Add to that a genuine love for souls, and a dash of "do unto others as..." But these solutions can not take the place of a better understanding of truth. It must not be equated with a few pat answers; or special attention to baptism, music, and "joining the church." We may feel our brethren are indoctrinated when in reality they know very little of fundamental principles of truth. Nor do we know denominational doctrine if we fail to understand the system back of those externals we often criticize.

Christianity is far more than slogans and flags to wave; yet, its principles do not require a D.D. or fancy theorizing. If we love souls, let us prepare our hearts to assist them.

From PLAIN TALK, March 1981, pg. 8

THE GOOD FIGHT

"I have fought the good fight, I have finished the course, I have kept the faith; in the future there is laid up for me the crown of righteousness, which the Lord, the righteous Judge, will award to me on that day ... "

— 2 Timothy 4:7-8

"Preach the word" seems like a rather straightforward and obvious request from Paul the teacher to Timothy the student. In fact, as Paul has already indicated in his letters to Timothy, preaching the word is not always easy. Sometimes it is a fight. Of course, it is always a fight against "the spiritual forces of wickedness" (Ephesians 6:12). But often it is a fight against flesh-and-blood people — sometimes, even against the people of God. Paul has already warned Timothy about so-called preachers who would try to substitute their own words and philosophies for those of God. Here, as he brings his letter to a close, he emphasizes how the listeners themselves will resist Timothy's efforts.

Sometimes the truth is "in season," sometimes it is "out of season" — that is, convenient and not convenient. Some people like to be reproved, rebuked and exhorted; others not. The latter would rather a preacher tickle their ears with pop psychology or promises of carnal blessings. A godly man will not give in to that sort of pressure, but instead will "finish the course."

The battle we face lasts as long as life lasts. We must find the courage to see it through to the end. "The faith" (Jude 3) will be opposed by many, including some who claim to be of "the faith." We must be prepared to engage the battle with such ones, wherever that battle may take place and whomever we may find ourselves facing. If we can endure to the end, God has a great reward waiting for us — "the crown of righteousness." This is the victory crown, awarded to all competitors who emerge from conflict as victorious over all comers. And unlike the games of old, all those "who have loved His appearing" will receive this crown. There is room on the medal stand for all of us.

Further Reading

Galatians 1:6-10

1 Corinthians 9:24-27

Hebrews 10:32-39

Why does Paul describe the faithful as "all who have loved His appearing"?

_____

_____

_____

Doug says ...

I am becoming discouraged. My roommate and I have had good discussions about the Bible ever since the college put us together. He seems sincere, but he genuinely does not understand the reason I emphasize what he considers "insignificant details." He is still willing to study, but I'm starting to wonder if I am wasting my time and his both.

What would you say to Doug?

_____

_____

_____

A Lesson from Your Bible—1 Samuel 17

When David appeared on the scene of the battle — the battle that seemed destined to never take place — he seemed genuinely puzzled that "this uncircumcised Philistine" would be able to taunt God's people in such a way without a response. His brother Eliab assumed he was just trying to insert himself in matters not of his concern; but then, Eliab had not accepted Goliath's challenge.

King Saul tried to discourage David from challenging the giant, who was a trained warrior besides. When he couldn't convince David to back away, he tried to give him his own armor — the armor Saul himself, apparently, was not willing to put on for the fight. Ironically, having someone to "go out before us and fight our battles" (1 Samuel 8:20) was one of the reasons Israel had clamored for a king in the first place. Now, with a king in place and a battle to fight, Saul was just as hesitant as everyone else.

David was willing and eager to take on Goliath because he knew the advantages enjoyed by Goliath meant nothing in a spiritual battle. Things such as physical strength, armament, and battle experience would have no impact on God — and it would be God, ultimately, who would be fighting the battle. It was David who slung the stone, but it was God who toppled the giant.

David knew the "good fight" was not the one he was likely to win, but rather the one that was worth fighting. God had granted David victory over lions and bears when he was tending sheep in the field, and he was confident God would give him victory over Goliath as well.

David would go on to write words of inspiration (including Psalm 3, Psalm 9, Psalm 10, and many other passages that relate directly to this sort of situation); we know at least that God had revealed His plan to make David king (1 Samuel 16:13). In any case, he was not content to sit back and simply pray, "Oh, that the salvation of Israel would come out of Zion!" (Psalm 14:7). He was determined to be the point of the spear in the hand of a righteous God.

Can we get too carried away with our confidence in God's victory, taking too many things for granted? Explain.

_____

_____

A Lesson from Your Elder

I have an aversion to fighting. I don't even like violent video games. But conflict is inevitable when you live in Satan's world. As it happens, fighting can be good, and even important. It shows what side of an issue you are on. It shows you how determined you are. It shows how far you will go in pursuit of a cause.

Don't be afraid to fight for your faith. Fight fairly, fight with integrity, fight according to the rules, but fight. Fight when you're winning. Fight when you're losing. Fight when you are surrounded by friends. Fight when you are surrounded by enemies. Fight when you are alone. Fight, and never stop.

I love you, and I'm praying for you.

> *O God and Father above,*
> *We live in a sinful world, full of sinful*
> *people who would pull us in and destroy*
> *us along with themselves. Help us love*
> *You, heaven, Your calling, the souls of our*
> *neighbors, to fight the good fight, finish*
> *the course, and keep the faith.*
> *In Jesus' name,*
> *Amen.*

From PLAIN TALK

"The Careless Ease of Fools"

Solomon wrote of a terrible day "when your fear cometh as a storm, and your calamity cometh on as a whirlwind." Those caught in such destruction had "despised reproof"; and were victims of "the careless ease of fools." (Prov. 1:24-33)

THE CARELESS EASE OF FOOLS ... give that some thought!! In N.T. times the same class of people are described as those who "will not endure sound doctrine; but wanting to have their ears tickled, they will accumulate for themselves teachers in accordance to their own desires" (2 Tim.4:3 N.A.S.). I am reminded of a recipient of PLAIN TALK who "Refused" the paper. When I inquired as to "Why?" she did not want the paper, she acknowledged that we were fair, had not hurt her feelings,-- and told the truth. But -- she "didn't like to read things like that." They made her uncomfortable.

If truth, fairly put, makes one uncomfortable; are we amiss in warning of "the careless ease of fools"?

Ours is a day of "careless ease"-- "eat, drink, and be merry!" When Solomon said it, he spoke of the vanity of life; and when Isaiah said it, he concluded, "for tomorrow we die." We want "liberty" to ignore right; "freedom" to run roughshod over our brethren; but there is neither liberty nor freedom in such a course. We are CREATURES -- and no head-in-the-sand policy can hide the fact that our only hope lies in acknowledging and serving our CREATOR.

We are confused. God's warnings are not judgement! He points up our sins, challenges our reckless course in an effort to prepare us for ultimate judgement. The gospel is God's power "unto salvation" (Rom.1:16) NOT unto damnation. God is "not willing that any should perish, but that all should come to repentance"(2 Pet.3:9).

The "ease" of those who ignore His word, who move merrily along with the majority, with "fun and frolic" for all, blinds them to the true joy and "peace that passeth understanding." With "the careless ease of fools" our nation, homes and souls are destroyed.

From PLAIN TALK, September 1966, pg. 1

REBELLIOUS MEN

"To the pure, all things are pure; but to those who are defiled and unbelieving, nothing is pure, but both their mind and their conscience are defiled."

— Titus 1:15

Stereotypes become stereotypes for a reason. That is not to say we can make a blanket judgment about a person's character based solely on his environment. But judging righteous judgment, as John 7:24 requires us to do, often involves taking environment into consideration.

Such was the case for Titus in Crete. The island nation's citizens had earned their reputation as "liars, evil beasts, lazy gluttons" (Titus 1:12). That did not mean that every Cretan Christian could be thus described. However, some could be; and Paul seemed to indicate he knew some of them to be well worthy of the description. And to make matters worse, they were infecting the church.

Titus' job as an evangelist was to oppose these rebellious men. His first task would be to appoint godly elders in every church. Apart from that, though, he was to continue to reprove the rebels. At stake were the rebels' own faith and the faith of those whom they would try to teach.

One of the defining traits of such men is their ability to turn good things into evil things. The Law of Moses was written by God, perfect for the task intended. Many Christians of Jewish heritage continued to live under the Law in good conscience. Some, though, put their faith in Moses rather than Jesus, saying Christians must submit to the Law to be saved (Acts 15:5). Beyond that, the Law was being used as a wedge to divide brethren. Saints with pure hearts could find the Lord with or without the Law, but "to those who are defiled and unbelieving, nothing is pure" (Titus 1:15). Even holy things can be used for the devil's purposes by those who only pretend to honor God.

Further Reading

Galatians 2:1-5

Romans 10:1-4

Philippians 3:17-21

How can it be said that troublemakers in the church deny God? _____

_____

_____

Erica says ...

I know Christians are supposed to give one another the benefit of the doubt. Love "believes all things." But it is really difficult with one person in my Bible class. He has been disruptive, disrespectful, rude, shallow and lazy ever since I've met him. He came forward a couple of weeks ago and confessed fault in a vague sort of way, but I don't see any change at all so far. What do I do?

What would you say to Erica?

_____

_____

_____

A Lesson from Your Bible—Acts 8:4-24

When Philip the evangelist brought the gospel to Samaria, in fulfillment of Jesus' own words (Acts 1:8), he met with great success. These souls who had some knowledge of the true God of heaven, though without the commitment to Him required in the Law of Moses, received Jesus as their Savior and put Him on in baptism. One of them was a remarkable fellow named Simon who had made a reputation for himself with what people called "the Great Power of God" (Acts 8:10). Whatever that "power" was, clearly it fell well short of the true power working through Philip; Simon responded to the gospel largely because even he was amazed at what Philip was doing.

(Some have cast doubt on Simon's sincerity. Only God can truly be the Judge of such things. However, Acts 8:13 clearly attaches Simon's faith to that of the rest of the Samaritan converts; it would seem that questioning Simon's conversion would call into question every other conversion in Samaria — and, indeed, every other example of working faith in the Bible.)

Soon afterward, Peter and John came from Jerusalem to visit with the new converts and to lay their hands on them, imparting gifts of the Holy Spirit. For Simon, this took the works of the Spirit to an entirely different level. To be able to do remarkable acts oneself was one thing; he had done similar things before knowing Jesus. But to empower others to do signs simply through the laying on of hands, this is something that staggered the imagination of Simon. Quickly he offered money to the apostles so that he, too, would be able to lay hands on believers and empower them. But Peter rebuked him, saying he was "in the gall of bitterness and in the bondage of iniquity" (Acts 8:23). There is no indication that the laying on of hands could be passed on at all; indeed, Peter and John's visit implies gifts of the Spirit could only be imparted by an apostle. But worse than merely misunderstanding the principles of authority, Simon demonstrated a carnal interest in spiritual things. Peter knew Simon wanted the power so he could be as important as Peter himself, not so he would be able to glorify Jesus and help his brethren.

Simon needed to repent, and he did — or, at least, he said he did. Modern carnal Christians need to repent as well.

How could a Christian use his or her standing in Christ for carnal gain?

_____

_____

A Lesson from Your Elder

Jesus comes first. Always. It is easy to prioritize yourself. Your friends and neighbors in the world do it, and they assume you do as well. You may even convince yourself that your selfish ambitions and your heavenly goals are compatible. But they are not.

No matter what you are doing in Jesus' name, it does not count toward your divine account unless you are doing it for Jesus' purposes. If He is not first, you are not right.

I love you, and I'm praying for you.

> *O God and Father above,*
> *We know there have always been*
> *rebellious men, empty talkers and*
> *deceivers among Your people. Help us*
> *to identify such ones, and especially to*
> *avoid becoming such ones. Help the next*
> *generation of believers be pure in heart,*
> *pure in doctrine, and pure in fellowship.*
> *In Jesus' name,*
> *Amen.*

From PLAIN TALK

Stuff About Things

Has anyone seen a plain, old-fashioned SINNER lately? They are getting mighty hard to find.

If the prodigal son were living today (as if he were not) he wouldn't be a SINNER. A juvenile delinquent perhaps; but his parents would be to blame for that. "There are no bad boys," you know. His wild oats are just youthful exuberance, a normal rebellion against unjust society, He must be free to "adjust positively."

There are no LIARS today. These fine people are simply extroverts, with imaginative talents that should be properly channeled. They evidence creative ability; their instability is a facet of their capacity for free uninhibited thought. They may become great poets, lawyers, -- or preachers.

The DRUNKARD is not really a sinner. He has an inferiority complex, and makes a mechanical adjustment (albeit a liquid one) to the problems of today. Besides that, he is sick. He beats his wife, starves his children, and is a scourge to society --- so he needs our sympathetic understanding.

ADULTERY may be sin in far-off slum districts; but not among movie stars, or popular public figures. And don't even mention the word when we get close to home. Here it is simply a case of biological maladjustment. The sex pervert was denied "free discussion" at home; his parents were old-fashioned and believed in common decency. His sin--er, I mean "mistake"— is a fault of modern society.

But maybe the MURDERER is a sinner -- just maybe! On the other hand, he may be the victim of some early traumatic experience. His mother was over-protective; he was greatly inhibited. He was never allowed to push his oats off the high-chair tray, so now he pushes his wife off Brooklyn Bridge. Poor fellow!

There may be an element of truth in all these descriptions; but one element, very necessary for correction, is lacking. We are overlooking the moral element.

Our generation needs psychiatry---but it also needs moral responsibility. We must recognize SIN for what it is-- SIN. We must cease to substitute Freud for Jesus Christ, the "Great Physician" who takes away the sins of the world. With the prodigal we must say, "I have SINNED!"

From PLAIN TALK, April 1964, pg. 8

SENSIBLE OLDER CHRISTIANS

"Older men are to be temperate, dignified, sensible, sound in faith, in love, in perseverance. Older women likewise are to be reverent ... so that the word of God will not be dishonored."

— Titus 2:2-5

"Act your age." How many times were you told that growing up? You probably thought it was an admonition given only to children. Actually, people of all ages have difficulty matching their behavior to their station in life. We cringe when a woman in her 50s insists on wearing clothing and hairstyles suited to teenagers. We chuckle at men in their 50s who buy sports cars. Are such things inherently shameful? Perhaps not. But when older ones pretend they are not old, they may be doing more than just reliving their youth; they may be rejecting the best parts of being old.

Older men, Paul writes, have learned how to act appropriately in different situations. They have learned to control their behavior. They have learned to detect, repel, and defend against false teaching. They have learned to persevere through hardships that may not evaporate in short order. None of these things is natural; it takes years of practice to hone these skills. Those who have had opportunity to do so, and who have properly taken advantage, are examples to the younger generation.

Older women have learned to avoid the flippant, gossipy behavior often associated with young girls. They know that the behavior of a godly woman — including things such as loving a husband or a child, which may seem automatic — are in fact skills to be mastered. Having progressed in these areas, they should make themselves available for younger ones who, despite what they may believe about themselves, have not had the opportunity to learn how to be a godly woman.

Pining away for lost youth is wasted effort. Instead, the elderly should rejoice at the opportunity to be the voices of experience for those who lack it.

Further Reading

1 Kiings 13

Proverbs
16:31; 20:29

Why do elderly people cringe at the idea of being perceived as old? _____

_____

_____

Doug says ...

I gave a fill-in sermon in the preacher's absence last week. The response was what I have come to expect — lots of people shaking my hand and telling me how wonderful it is to see young people doing what I do. One man didn't much like my way of talking about grace, and he said so. Maybe I'm being difficult to please, but I feel like the older generation is talking down to me either way.

What would you say to Doug?

_____

_____

_____

A Lesson from Your Bible—2 Chronicles 24

The reign of Joash started in a remarkable way, to say the least. His father, Ahaziah, was killed in the purge of Ahab's family. (Ahaziah's father, Jehoram, had married Ahab's daughter, Athaliah.) Athaliah tried to have the rest of her family killed as well so as to reign in Judah herself. But Ahaziah's son Joash, who was just a small child, managed to survive. Eventually Joash's mentor, Jehoiada the priest, was able to put the 7-year-old on the throne and bring about the death of Athaliah.

Jehoiada provided important counsel to the young king. Through his influence the temple was repaired and provisions were put in place for its continual upkeep. Joash remained a noble and godly king until Jehoiada's death at the age of 130.

Things quckly changed, though, after that. Other counselors were able to convince Joash to abandon his reformer ways and abandon God to serve idols. Zechariah, the son of Jehoiada, was moved by the Spirit to oppose Joash. He condemned his actions in front of the people. Joash and his new advisors had Zechariah stoned right there in the court of the temple. But before he died, Zechariah pronounced a curse: "May the LORD see and avenge!"

God heard the plea of His righteous one. Judah suffered a crushing defeat at the hands of the Arameans. Soon afterward, the already-sickly Joash was assassinated by rebels who were horrified at his fall from God's grace and his treatment of Zechariah.

Exactly how old Joash was when Jehoiada died is difficult to determine from the text. What we do know is, Jehoiada was able to serve an important role prior to and during Joash's reign, often against great opposition. The impact he had for good lasted well beyond the death of those who tried to undo it.

How much responsibility does one generation have in molding and guiding the next generation?

_____

_____

A Lesson from Your Elder

I have entered into my second half-century of life here on earth. I don't act like I did when I was young. Part of that is because I am incapable of doing so. But mostly (so far, at least) it is by choice. The things that delighted me a few decades ago, which are very similar to the things that delight you, don't have the same attraction anymore. If you'll pardon me for sounding condescending, I grew up.

I may show some distaste, or even contempt, for some of your pastimes. If so, you can accuse me of forgetting what it is like to be young. And you may have a fair point. But perhaps you should consider that you have never known what it is to be old. So perhaps it is you who is having trouble relating to me, and not the other way around.

I love you, and I'm praying for you.

> *O God and Father above,*
> *Bless the older generation of Christians*
> *that remains. Help them deal with the*
> *younger generations with kindness,*
> *patience and love. Help them rejoice in*
> *their maturity and experience. Help them*
> *value it so that younger ones will value it*
> *as well, and seek it out as a source of wis-*
> *dom and guidance.*
> *In Jesus' name,*
> *Amen.*

From PLAIN TALK

A Christian Is Sober

Ours is an age which puts emphasis upon the off-beat, weight upon that which is flimsy and light. We are easily "caught up" in this trend; so the straight line becomes more and more rare, even on the most serious subjects. But Christianity is no joke, and the Christian must learn seriousness, at the risk of being thought a "square" (or the modern equivalent).

Paul told Titus (1:8) a bishop must be sober, just, holy, temperate. That word "sober" does not refer to freedom from alcohol, primarily; but calls for a certain state of mind or attitude -- sometimes translated "sensible." The Greek is "sophron," a combine of "save" and "mind." A "soundminded" person exercises common sense, is not a radical, is discreet. It is easy to see how this would be a necessary qualification for an overseer.

But when Paul tells Titus to teach the things which become sound doctrine (Titus 2:1-f) he lists the need for aged men to be "sober, grave, temperate"; the later from "sophron" and meaning "soberminded" or "sensible". The older women are to teach the younger women to be sober, or "discrete." Titus is to exhort young men to be "sober-minded" (again, from our word "sophron"); and Titus is to do his teaching with "gravity."

In the more general passage of Rom. 12:3 we are told not to think more highly of ourselves than we ought to think, "but to think soberly, according as God hath dealt to every man the measure of faith." Apparently this "sober" attitude is a sort of antidote and antithesis of one of our greatest faults, egotism. In the past various religions have made a "long face" the sign of piety, so that laughter was practically a sin. The same spirit was reflected in clothing, which must be drab, unattractive, and out of style. I believe these extremes often resulted in folk taking "pride" in their very lack of conformity, so that their garb and conduct became symbols of godliness "to be seen of men" rather than the genuine article. But this could not be charged against them all; nor can we deny that today's so-called Christian who is giddy with foolishness, and slave to silly fashions, makes a fool of himself and violates God's exhortation to be sober, sensible.

This will not set well with some of today's church-members, but I believe it should be said. A Christian is conservative in dress and manner, and cannot take the lead in fashion and "continental" foolishness. Today's absurdities may become tomorrow's norm (although "fads" seldom get such general acceptance) but if they do, I believe a Christian should wait for tomorrow, even for those practices morally right within themselves. (We assume that if you have read this far you know we would not advocate participation in a thing wrong within itself, no matter how stylish.)

A Christian is concerned primarily with salvation of the soul. Thoughts are upon "things above, not on things on the earth." (Col .3:2) "The end of all things is at hand: be ye therefore sober, and watch unto prayer" (1 Pet.4:7). JUDGEMENT WILL SOBER US!!

From PLAIN TALK, October 1967, pg. 4

SENSIBLE YOUNGER CHRISTIANS

"Likewise urge the young men to be sensible; in all things show yourself to be an example of good deeds, with purity in doctrine, dignified"

— Titus 2:6-7

There is a tendency to allow young people to "act like young people." Sometimes that involves behavior that is somewhat outrageous or edgy, such as skydiving or getting a crazy haircut. Sometimes it is behavior that is dangerous or sinful. Clearly there is a difference. In either case, though, it is not enough to simply overlook inappropriate behavior in young people, assuming they will "grow out of it." The mandate for older Christians to be "sensible" applies to younger Christians as well. That doesn't mean they can't have fun or that they must act twice their age. It does mean, though, they should have more on their mind than just the next good time.

As Paul mentioned to Timothy (1 Timothy 4:11-13), the influence of younger saints is important. Mistakes made through youthful impulses can be remembered for a lifetime, and be held against the entire body as well as the individual. Pleas for offended ones to "lighten up" in such matters are generally ignored; in fact, it is likely that time makes the infraction seem worse instead of better.

However unreasonable it may seem (and sometimes it seems very much so), we need to take others' reactions and potential reactions into consideration when we are choosing a course of action. It is easy for young people to think only of himself, or to assume bad reactions will be manageable, or that their ability to justify themselves in their own minds is the only "judging" that should be permitted. But that is, if you will pardon the bluntness, an immature way of looking at things. Children think that way because they are incapable of thinking any other way. If a young man or woman is self-aware and mature enough to choose to serve Jesus Christ, he or she is able to mimic Jesus' attitude of selflessness and sacrifice.

Further Reading

Ecclesiastes
11:9-10

Philippians 2:4-5

1 Peter 2:9-12

At what point can we consider ourselves "beyond reproach"? _____

_____

_____

Erica says ...

I was raised to stay away from "the line" where behavior becomes sinful. I know there are judgment calls to be made, but there is also "righteous judgment." Some of the Christian friends I have made since leaving home seem to take great pleasure in getting as close to the line as possible. They call it having fun. At what point do I stop being careful and become a prude?

What would you say to Erica?

_____

_____

_____

A Lesson from Your Bible—Esther 4

The story of Esther is a case study in providence. As has often been stated, you don't see God's name in the book but you do see His hand. A young woman finds herself in a position where she could effect the salvation of her entire nation — or, perhaps, die in the attempt. Extraordinary circumstances reveal the hero or coward in each of us. Such was the case for Esther.

After having married the king and been welcomed into his life and confidence, Esther hears through her cousin Mordecai that plans are in the works to destroy all the Jews — not only in the Persian capital of Susa, where they lived, but throughout the empire. A man named Haman, driven by his personal animosity toward Mordecai, had made it his mission in life to have his vengeance and have it manifold.

Esther, as had been the case throughout her life, leaned on Mordecai for advice. He pointed out that she had an opportunity to demonstrate courage and perhaps accomplish something great. He told her, "For if you remain silent at this time, relief and deliverance will arise for the Jews from another place and you and your father's house will perish. And who knows whether you have not attained royalty for such a time as this?"

Esther could have ignored the warning signs. She could have trusted in her relationship with the king to save her and perhaps her cousin, ignoring the threat to others. But she had the wisdom to respect and defer to the wisdom of one more experienced than she.

The faith of Mordecai was rock-solid. He knew God had plans for the Jews and that Haman would not be able to completely derail them. But he also knew the people of God are not passive participants in His process. By respecting the judgment of someone older and wiser, Esther was able to choose a path for her life that led her to become an example of faith herself.

Is advice from older people always good? How can we tell one way or the or the other?

_____

_____

A Lesson from Your Elder

Every older person you have ever met used to be a younger person. You probably struggle to believe that in some cases (like me), but I promise it's true. And speaking for most of us, we are not trying to cramp your style, clip your wings, or douse your spirit. We're just trying to help you find your way through life with fewer self-inflicted wounds than we experienced.

We recognize that you need to be left to make your own mistakes, to an extent. Please be patient with us as we try (and sometimes struggle) to be patient with you.

I love you, and I'm praying for you.

> *O God and Father above,*
> *We praise you for your love and mercy.*
> *We thank you for the opportunities you*
> *give us to learn from our mistakes, and to*
> *serve you more effectively as a result.*
> *Please help our young people, and our*
> *not-so-young ones as well, be humble*
> *enough to receive your chastening.*
> *In Jesus' name,*
> *Amen.*

From *PLAIN TALK*

Stuff About Things

When I was a student in Freed-Hardeman College, the President of that institution was wont to say (in jest I trust), "He that tooteth not his own horn, the same shall not be tooted!" It brought a laugh from the many "preacher boys" — albeit a nervous laugh, for we were a "heady" bunch.

Maybe one of those boys was the chief character in a recent happening. Someone asked this (unnamed) preacher if he was the greatest preacher in the brotherhood. He said, "No, but I would have to be numbered among the top two; and I'm more humble than the other fellow."

My informant did not tell me of a retort, if there was one; but that remark deserved something like one given a certain sportscaster. He is reported to have asked another how many truly great sportscasters there were for today's football games, and the man replied, "I don't know the number, but there is one less than you think." Wow! That smarts!

And so it goes. We are repulsed by the fellow who "thinks more highly of himself than he ought to think" (Rom. 12:3). It is barely possible that his attitude is obnoxious because it is an indirect attack upon our status — whittling us down by the unwarranted elevation of himself. And how many of us have tried to measure how highly "we ought to think" (v. 3b)? "Soberly" suggests an unexaggerated, objective look at ourselves, "according as God hath dealt to every man the measure of faith;" but it does not require nor promote a loss of self-respect. God has dealt each one "a measure of faith," and each saint should be sufficiently aware of his "measure" to recognize his responsibilities. Our various capacities pose corresponding obligations. Let no one excuse his failure to serve the Lord under the guise of false modesty.

The egoist leads a self-centered life. His philosophy makes self-interest the valid end of all action. He must "justify himself" (Lu. 10:29) at whatever the cost. The self-sacrificing love of Christianity negates such an attitude as this. Christ did not undersell himself, but gladly gave himself for others (Jn. 8:28, 12:32). We also have a purpose and a God-given function to perform. We cannot serve well with either an over — or an under-inflated concept of self. But a true look at self will make us aware of our need for Christ, saying, "Be merciful to me, a sinner!"

From PLAIN TALK, January 1979, pg. 8

SENSIBLE LIVING

"For the grace of God has appeared, bringing salvation to all men, instructing us to deny ungodliness and worldly desires and to live sensibly, righteously, and godly in this present age"

— Titus 2:11-12

Already in Titus 2, Paul has instructed young and old alike to be "sensible." But what does it really mean to live a "sensible" life? That would depend on what "sense" you are following, it would seem. For a person living apart from God, focusing only on this life, the "sensible" thing would be to enhance one's own short-term and long-term physical pleasure. Being physical beings ourselves, we as Christians can appreciate that mentality; to an extent, we share it.

But as Christians, "looking for the blessed hope," we have more "sense" than to limit ourselves to this life. Indeed, we realize this life ultimately is about demonstrating ourselves "a people for His own possession, zealous for good deeds." Therefore the most "sensible" thing we could do is push back against the tide of worldliness we see around us, choosing instead to live for heaven.

The existence of the grace of God in our lives, the salvation we enjoy, necessarily requires us to live differently from those on the outside. Sinning the more that grace might increase (Romans 6:1-2) is a hateful thought to the one who looks to Jesus.

The appeal of "worldly desires" is real, but fleshly. I may feel like a diet of only ice cream will feel good in the moment, and it will; however, a sensible person will realize the short-term and long-term consequences of that choice. In the same way, the sensible thing for a Christian to do "in this present age" is to prepare for heaven. Jesus says in Luke 16:10, sandwiched between two stories about stewardship, "He who is faithful in a very little thing is faithful also in much; and he who is unrighteous in a very little thing is unrighteous also in much." May we have the good sense to learn that lesson.

Further Reading

Ephesians 5:15-16

1 Peter 4:1-6

Luke 16:1-13, 19-31

Describe in your own words what "makes sense" about being a Christian.

_____

_____

_____

Doug says ...

The concept of "slippery slopes" is troublesome to me. You could eliminate anything based on the idea that it might lead to something bad. Weddings in the church building might lead to instruments in one of those weddings, and before you know it the church is buying a piano (just for weddings), and then one day the church is conducting an instrumental worship service. Sorry, I just don't buy it.

What would you say to Doug?

_____

_____

_____

A Lesson from Your Bible—Matthew 25:1-13

Jesus had a great deal to say about preparation, particularly toward the end of His ministry. A cluster of stories and illustrations are recorded for us in Matthew 24-25. The specific context is the coming destruction of Jerusalem at the hands of the Romans. But the principles of preparation have application in many other areas. We are constantly being judged by the Lord, including at times of great stress and challenge. The application to end-time events and final judgment is obviously in view as well. There will come a time, as describe in 2 Peter 3:3-9, when all will stand before the Lord and give account. The time to prepare for judgment is not the day of judgment itself; we must make preparations ahead of time — and as early and completely as possible.

One of Jesus' stories involves ten virgins awaiting a marriage feast in which they had been invited to participate. Their task was to simply wait with oil lamps burning until the bridegroom arrived. Five of them took the extra measure of bringing another supply of oil with them; five took no extra oil, only what was in the lamps. Unfortunately for the second group, the bridegroom did not arrive on schedule. The delay depleted their supply of oil and forced them to go find more; while they were gone, the bridegroom arrived, the prudent five virgins entered into the feast, "and the door was shut" (v.10) — surely some of the most final words to be found in Scripture. No amount of begging or excuse-making could get the door opened again for the ones who were not quite as prepared as they should have been.

Often it has been asked whether it would have been appropriate and kind of the one group to lend from their surplus to the other group. The answer comes back, perhaps. But this is a story about preparation, not kindness. Jesus was not suggesting we should be hoarders of His gifts. He was simply pointing out that some preparations cannot be made by proxy. We cannot get ready to stand before the Lord by getting others to prepare on our behalf. We must bring our own oil.

What can we do today to prepare for final judgment?

_____

_____

A Lesson from Your Elder

People used to think before they acted back in my day. They had to. Acting took time and preparation. By the time you got around to it, you couldn't help but have thought about the action for a bit. Today is different. With the internet and social media, you can act with virtually no thought at all. But it's kind of like putting hot fudge on your French fries; just because you can doesn't mean you should.

The internet is forever. The stunt you think is so hysterical right now may be hurtful to someone else, and one day embarrassing to you. So imagine what it might look like when you are looking back at it from 20 years in the future. not just in terms of right now. That process is why I don't have an O.J. Simpson tattoo today.

I love you, and I'm praying for you.

> *O God and Father above,*
> *When we think about the decisions we*
> *have to make and the consequences they*
> *may bring, it staggers us to think how little*
> *control we have over the world around us.*
> *Help us exercise whatever control we may*
> *with the wisdom that You provide.*
> *In Jesus' name,*
> *Amen.*

From PLAIN TALK

Tempus Fugit

One need not know Latin to know "time flies;" but awareness of its fleeting nature seems reserved for the older. So we were intrigued by a teaching method introduced into a young people's class in Arkansas. The instructor asked the students to say to themselves, "I am now 20 years older" — and then try to imagine where I will live, how I will look, what will be my circumstances.

After the first wave of foolishness wears away, and the class begins to think as realistically as possible, the teacher leads them to ask', "What kind of wife or husband I want," or, "Will I be capable of handling a good job?" Obviously the youngsters cannot be "matured" instantaneously, but with proper guidance they can get a glimpse of what lays ahead. And when attitudes seem right, the teacher begins to inquire about spiritual goals and relate high ideals, principles of Christ, to the good life here, and to the life hereafter. How do you want your children to behave, and how can you guide them to know what you know? Skillful use of this tactic can produce useful introspection — and seeing ourselves is a tremendous step toward self-improvement. Future time can be better realized by comparing it to past time. Looking back, 5 years seems very brief; yet the future 5 years have exactly the same number of hours: only then we will be __ years old; and how better prepared to meet our Maker?

I remember telling a girl who was not particularly enthusiastic about finishing school: "Five years from now you could be a widow with two small children to support." It seems ridiculous to youth — but Oh how real it can become, and Oh so soon.

"Wherefore he saith, Awake thou that sleepest, and arise from the dead, and Christ shall shine upon thee. Look therefore carefully how ye walk, not as unwise, but as wise; redeeming the time, because the days are evil" (Eph. 5:14-16). "Redeeming the time" is "buying up the opportunity" in footnote. We only have NOW for certain, and what we do NOW will determine our future. So very soon NOW will be our past opportunity.

From PLAIN TALK, April 1982, pg. 1

FACTIOUSNESS

"Reject a factious man after a first and second warning, knowing that such a man is perverted and is sinning, being self-condemned."

— Titus 3:10-11

When Titus is quoted, it is generally for one of two purposes: defining the character of an elder, and condemning factiousness. But both really speak to the topic of leadership in the Lord's church — how it is implemented, and how it is followed. There are always going to be those who push back against authority, whether it be civil authority, parental authority, divine authority or congregational authority. We are naturally willful beings. We like getting our way. We dislike yielding in judgment to others. But if we have difficulty yielding in matters regarding human authority figures, how can we possibly learn to yield to our invisible Savior?

The obvious difference between divine authority and human authority is that human authority is flawed. People make mistakes, and that includes authority figures. It is not uncommon for those who think themselves to be important or knowledgeable to assert themselves for what they might call the greater good. Such ones are ignorant of the fact that learning to submit to authority generally is the greater good.

Persisting in public rebellion cannot be tolerated. Paul emphasizes in chapter 3 the "foolish" nature of our lives outside of Christ and the transformation Jesus is supposed to have made in us. If we obsess over points of difference — not emphasizing actual Biblical teaching but rather our own application of it — to the point of acquiring a following, we are guilty of fragmenting the church. Just as moral error must be exposed and expunged (1 Corinthians 5), so also must we remove the false teacher among us. And remember, "false" in this context need not be factually incorrect. Obsessing over "foolish controversies and genealogies and strife and disputes about the Law" is intolerable when it reaches the point of turning a man into the leader of a faction.

Further Reading

1 Corinthians
1:10-17;
3:1-9

Ephesians 4:1-6

Explain the "washing of regeneration and renewing by the Holy Spirit (v. 5). _____

_____

_____

Erica says ...

The elders discussed selling the church property and relocating in a meeting with the men a few weeks ago. Soon afterward, the elders announced not to sell. That night I had a date with the young man who brought up the topic. He was furious. He laid out his whole plan, detailing why the elders were wrong and what his next step would be. I was extremely uncomfortable.

What would you say to Erica?

_____

_____

_____

A Lesson from Your Bible—2 Samuel 15

The rise and fall of Absalom accomplished God's plan for the chastening of David, as prophesied by Nathan in 2 Samuel 12:11 after David's sin with Bathsheba. So it would be fair to say Absalom was helped along by the Lord in his attempt to steal the kingdom from his father. Even so, it is difficult to ignore the fact that David could have stopped Absalom at any point during this process with a bit of forethought, insight, or even just garden-variety paying attention to the young man.

Absalom clearly had been angry with his father since David refused to act against Amnon, Absalom's half-brother, when he defiled Absalom's sister Tamar. We read in 2 Samuel 13-14 how Absalom eventually killed his brother and fled the kingdom, and how David received him back but ignored him, and how eventually they were reconciled. But clearly, all had not been forgiven for Absalom.

Day by day, Absalom sowed seeds of discord among the people. He presented himself as a preferred alternative to his father, telling lies about him to all who would hear. Eventually, enough of the people and of David's close advisers came over to Absalom's side that David was forced to flee for his life. Eventually, the lives of 20,000 men were lost (2 Samuel 18:7), including Absalom's own life.

David's checkered history with Absalom, no doubt, caused him to deal with Absalom lightly; perhaps, at first, this was not a poor notion. But as it became more and more obvious what Absalom's ultimate intentions were, David's passivity becomes inexcusable. Either he simply was not paying attention to his son (a problem for David throughout his reign), or he was afraid his interaction would somehow make things worse instead of better. But fear of failure is no justification for leaving needful activity undone.

David and the entire nation, including Absalom himself, paid a dear penalty because of David's failure. David did a great many things in his life that deserve our praise and imitation. His treatment of Absalom was not one of those things.

What is the best way for elders to keep factiousness from ever becoming a problem? What is the best way for us to avoid becoming factious ourselves?

_____

_____

_____

A Lesson from Your Elder

Paul writes in 1 Corinthians 3:17, "If any man destroys the temple of God, God will destroy him." Does that sound serious to you? It sounds very serious to me.

Situations arise, more's the pity, when battle lines must be drawn and sides must be chosen. Such was the case in my father's day and in my day, and it will be in your day as well. Make double-sure you are fighting for God's way and not your own way.

I love you, and I'm praying for you.

> *O God and Father above,*
> *We thank you for the wisdom you have*
> *shown us in giving us local fellowships of*
> *brethren. We see Your face in our breth-*
> *ren. The strength they give us is Your*
> *strength. We rejoice in this foretaste of*
> *heaven, and we give you all the praise.*
> *Please give us and our fellow Christians*
> *the humility we need to accept Your direc-*
> *tion for local churches. Help us participate*

*in the building of a temple worthy of the
name of Your Son.
Help us identify Diotrephes among us,
and help us find the courage to repent
when his spirit is in our hearts. Let us
serve no lord, but Jesus, no cause but His
cause.
In Jesus' name,
Amen.*

From PLAIN TALK

Stuff About Things

While in Australia, Phil Morr had the hair-curling experience of riding with a man who, late in life, had but recently completed a driver-training course. He had learned to start a car by methodical steps, followed explicitly: viz., place feet firmly on the floor, engage emergency brake, check gears, turn key, etc. At a traffic light the engine died, and he had to go through each "step" to restart it; only to kill it again upon release of the clutch. Horns honked, traffic piled up, as the procedure began anew.

Finally the car was started again, but by now the light had changed and heavy traffic was zipping across in front of them. The beginner had the car in gear, then, seeing the traffic he became confused and pressed hard upon both clutch and accelerator. The motor roared, the car shook, and the driver looked beseechingly to Phil for instructions. To his everlasting credit, and well being, Phil said calmly, "George, don't do anything until you have lifted your foot from the ACCELERATOR." (Emphasis, PHIL)

What a world of wisdom those words convey when applied to critical problems in our own lives. The argument heats up, confusion reigns, the very foundations seem to shake — and what shall we do? "George, don't do anything until you have lifted your foot from the ACCELERATOR!"

"For lack of wood the fire goeth out" (Prov. 26:20). That does not mean all troubles will cease if left alone for it continues, "And where there is no whisperer, contention ceaseth." It says we may fuel contentions by gossip and unwise comments. Unwittingly, we may stir to a white heat the very thing we would like to squelch. Some may become aware they are stirring a hornet's nest to no good end, but pride and "position" are committed, and they will go down with the ship (taking others with them) before letting up on the gas. How very sad!!

Somehow we have imagined a correlation between strength and loudness; between soundness and sharp retort. Of course, soft-spoken talk of love does not make a thing right, and we freely admit it "gets on our nerve" when we know it covers error. But Christlike treatment will not foster error, and it may avoid a fatal wreck.

From PLAIN TALK, March 1982, pg. 8

Made in the USA
Middletown, DE
22 June 2019